# The Operating Partner Playbook:

# A Comprehensive Guide to

# Total Value Creation® in

# Private Equity

By

Mohamad Chahine

February 2024

*First Edition*

**MeritIP Publishing**

**"The only safe ship in a storm is leadership."**

*"Mastering value creation is key; it is not the strongest of the industries that survive, nor the most intelligent, but the ones most responsive to change. **The Operating Partner Playbook** is your compass in navigating the ever-evolving landscapes of private equity and requirements for operational excellence, where the true north lies in the relentless pursuit of innovation and strategic partnerships."*

# Expanded Table of Contents

# Introduction

Welcome to "The Operating Partner Playbook: A Comprehensive Guide to Total Value Creation in Private Equity," your trusted companion on the journey towards enhancing operational value creation in the world of private equity.

This comprehensive guide is designed to provide industry veterans, aspiring investment professionals, corporate executives, and curious entrepreneurs with valuable insights and practical strategies to drive success in the ever-evolving landscape of private equity.

In today's dynamic business environment, operational expertise has emerged as a critical differentiator, playing a pivotal role in maximizing returns and driving growth within portfolio companies. This book serves as your roadmap, offering a treasure trove of knowledge, best practices, and innovative frameworks to boost operational performance and create sustainable value.

Throughout my career, which I describe as a full loop from Operations, Consulting, Private Equity, and back to Operations, I had the privilege of working with many bright and hard-working professionals. These individuals became my mentors, and my interactions with them, along with many other dedicated and experienced private equity practitioners, helped me cultivate a deep understanding of the intricacies and challenges faced by operational partners and investment professionals. By collaborating with industry leaders, conducting extensive research, and compiling years of real-world insights, I have taken my first step to craft a comprehensive and purposeful guide that empowers aspiring investment professionals and advisors to unlock the true potential of their investment efforts and resources.

Besides sharing a detailed overview of the PE industry and mapping the Operating Partners' roles and responsibilities, my primary goal in writing this book was to identify, develop, and propose a purposeful and tested framework to streamline and optimize value creation. This framework, named the Value Management System, is intended to be universal and helpful not only in Private Equity settings but across the wide spectrum of asset management, from entrepreneurship and startups to venture capital, SMEs, and asset management. This is not intended to be a buzzword but rather a genuine umbrella of tools and frameworks that promote both innovation and discipline in the value creation cycle. Be prepared to receive a plethora of original concepts and insights. You might agree with many and disagree with others, but nonetheless, both outcomes pave the way for my point that investment leaders need to treat the practice of Operational Value Creation (OVC) with more rigor and insights. Thought Leadership is and remains the cornerstone of sustainable value creation.

Within these pages, we delve deep into the merit-driven Value Management System (mVMS), a groundbreaking framework designed to revolutionize the way value is created and managed in private equity. By integrating strategic planning, operational efficiency, talent management, risk mitigation, innovation, and more, mVMS offers a comprehensive approach that enhances portfolio company performance holistically.

My goal is not simply to provide theoretical concepts but to offer practical solutions that can be applied directly in your day-to-day operations. From understanding the economic implications of operational partnerships to quantifying performance gaps, we leave no stone unturned, ensuring that you have the tools and knowledge to drive operational excellence and maximize value creation.

Throughout this book, we also explore the critical role of operational partners, who act as catalysts for value creation within portfolio companies. We decipher the diverse involvement models of operational partners, emphasizing the importance of talent acquisition and retention strategies, the integration of Environmental, Social, and Governance (ESG) responsibilities, and the resolution of industry-specific challenges through tailored solutions.

Additionally, we recognize the transformative impact of technology in the private equity landscape. With the advent of Industry 4.0 and the rise of automation, we explore how technological advancements are reshaping

**8**

traditional investment paradigms. This includes insights into leveraging artificial intelligence, automation, and data analytics to unlock untapped potential and drive value across industries.

To ensure optimal organization and appeal to our diverse readership, this book is divided into three key sections:

PART 1: A Primer on Private Equity – The Primal yet Obscure Asset Class - delves into the diverse aspects of Private Equity, exploring the investment process, stages, roles, and functions.

PART 2: A Primer on The Operating Partner in the PE World - delves into the critical aspects of operational partnerships, exploring their role, involvement models, talent management strategies, and industry-specific challenges.

PART 3: The Merit-driven Value Management System Solution - provides an in-depth analysis of our innovative framework, mVMS, designed to revolutionize value creation. This section offers practical insights and guidance on strategic planning, operational efficiency, talent management, risk mitigation, innovation, and more.

This book is not only a comprehensive guide but also a catalyst for change, inspiring a paradigm shift in how we approach value creation within private equity. By sharing this knowledge and providing you with the necessary tools, I believe that you can unlock the full potential of your investments, build resilient portfolio companies, and leave a lasting impact in the ever-evolving landscape of private equity.

So, join me on this enriching journey as we explore operational value creation in private equity. Together, let's unlock the true potential, transcend industry boundaries, and lay the foundation for operational excellence as the cornerstone of success.

# PART 1 :

# A Primer on Private Equity
## The Primal yet Obscure Asset Class

# Understanding Private Equity

### Introduction

Private Equity (PE) has evolved into a dynamic and influential asset class, attracting investors seeking superior returns and active involvement in shaping the destiny of portfolio companies. This comprehensive primer dives into the rationale, processes, key players, strategies, risks, valuation methods, and recent trends that define the world of Private Equity.

Why Private Equity?

### Enhanced Returns and Active Ownership

Investors are drawn to Private Equity for its unique advantages. Unlike public markets, PE offers the opportunity for direct ownership, allowing investors to wield influence over strategic decisions and actively participate in value creation. This direct engagement often translates to superior returns compared to traditional investment avenues.

### Diversification

PE investments provide a diversification avenue, reducing the correlation with traditional asset classes. This diversification not only helps in mitigating risk but also allows investors to tap into a different set of industries and geographies.

### Long-Term Perspective

PE funds typically operate with a longer investment horizon, aligning the interests of investors and portfolio companies for sustained growth. This long-term perspective enables strategic decision-making that may be constrained in public markets driven by short-term shareholder expectations.

**Asset Class Overview**

Private Equity comprises various investment strategies, each tailored to specific business life cycles.

### 1. Venture Capital (VC)

VC involves early-stage funding for startups with high growth potential. Venture capitalists provide capital to fuel innovation, with a focus on emerging technologies and groundbreaking ideas.

### 2. Growth Equity

Growth Equity investments target established companies poised for expansion. This strategy involves injecting capital into companies with proven business models to accelerate growth and innovation.

### 3. Buyouts

Buyouts entail acquiring controlling stakes in mature companies. Private Equity firms employ restructuring and operational improvements to enhance the performance of these companies, aiming for significant value appreciation. The term LBO (Leveraged Buyouts) is very common.

### 4. Special Situations

Special Situation investments cover a broad spectrum, including distressed assets, turnarounds, and unique market opportunities. This strategy allows PE firms to capitalize on specific market conditions and inefficiencies.

# The Private Equity Process

The private equity (PE) investment process is a methodical journey encompassing origination, due diligence, deal execution, value creation, and harvesting/realization.

1. **Origination**

   Origination is the initial phase where private equity firms identify and source potential investment opportunities. This involves scouting for companies that align with the investment criteria and strategy of the PE firm.

2. **Due Diligence**

   Due diligence is a meticulous evaluation of the identified investment opportunities. This process entails comprehensive assessments of the target company's financial health, operational efficiency, market positioning, and associated risks. It serves as a crucial step in making informed investment decisions.

3. **Deal Execution**

   Upon successful due diligence, the deal execution phase begins. This involves finalizing the terms of the investment, conducting legal procedures, and completing the transaction. Deal execution is pivotal for formally establishing the private equity firm's ownership in the portfolio company.

4. **Value Creation**

   After acquiring a stake in the portfolio company, private equity firms actively participate in its operations. The value creation phase focuses on implementing strategic initiatives to enhance the company's overall value. This may include operational optimizations, expansion strategies, innovation, and other value-enhancing measures.

## 5. Harvesting/Realization

The ultimate objective of a private equity investment is to realize returns for investors. The harvesting/realization phase involves executing exit strategies, such as Initial Public Offerings (IPOs), secondary sales, mergers, or acquisitions. This critical phase is essential for converting the increased value of the portfolio companies into tangible monetary returns for the private equity firm and its investors.

# Private Equity Fund Structure

The structure of a Private Equity fund is fundamental to understanding the dynamics of the asset class.

### Open-End and Closed-End Funds

Private Equity funds can be structured as open-end or closed-end. Open-end funds allow investors to enter or exit the fund at any time, while closed-end funds have a fixed maturity period, typically ranging from seven to ten years.

### Mandate, Hurdle Rate, and Carried Interest

A Private Equity fund operates under a specific mandate, outlining the fund's focus, investment strategy, and sector preferences. The hurdle rate is the minimum rate of return that must be achieved before the fund managers can receive carried interest—a share of the profits. Typical Hurdle Rate of 8% -10% and Carried Interest of 20% (on a compounded basis).

### Management Fee and Key Personnel

Private Equity funds charge a management fee, usually a percentage of committed capital, to cover operational expenses. Key Personnel, including General Partners (GPs) and investment professionals, play a crucial role in the success of the fund.

# Access to Private Equity

Investors can access Private Equity through various channels, each offering different levels of involvement.

### 1. Direct Investment

Direct investment involves acquiring ownership directly in private companies. This approach provides maximum control and allows investors to directly influence the operations and strategic decisions of the portfolio company.

## 2. Primary Investment

Primary investments involve committing capital to Private Equity funds managed by experienced General Partners. Investors become Limited Partners in these funds, gaining exposure to a diversified portfolio managed by the PE firm.

## 3. Secondary Investments

Secondary investments involve purchasing existing Private Equity fund stakes from other investors. This approach allows investors to enter established funds and gain exposure to a mature portfolio of assets.

# PE Lifecycle and Mechanisms

Navigating the private equity landscape involves understanding the intricacies of the investment timeline. Key elements, such as holding periods, vintage considerations, and the distribution waterfall, play pivotal roles in shaping the journey of private equity funds. This exploration will delve into three main sections: the lifespan of a private equity fund, mechanisms governing capital flows, and critical events influencing fund dynamics.

**Lifespan of a Private Equity Fund**

*Holding Period:* The holding period, a cornerstone of private equity, typically spans several years. Investments are made with a long-term perspective, and holding periods can range from 5 to 10 years. This extended duration allows fund managers to implement value creation strategies and optimize portfolio performance before considering exits.

*Vintage and Sunset:* Vintage years denote the period of fund inception, influencing its characteristics. Funds raised during economic upturns may have distinct performance traits compared to those raised during downturns. Sunset, on the other hand, marks the end of the fund's investment phase, usually occurring around the 5 to 7-year mark. Post-sunset, the focus shifts to maximizing returns from existing investments.

*Wind Down:* The wind-down phase signifies the conclusion of a fund's lifecycle, typically occurring around the 10-year mark. During this period, the fund systematically exits remaining investments, and proceeds are distributed to investors. A well-executed wind-down ensures a smooth conclusion to the fund's operations.

**Mechanisms Governing Capital Flows**

*Equity Call:* Equity calls are strategic capital-raising moments during the fund's life. Investors, or limited partners, fulfill capital commitments when called upon by the fund manager. These calls often take place in the initial years, aligning with the fund's deployment phase.

*Clawbacks and Distribution Waterfall:* Clawbacks act as safeguards for fair profit distribution. If early profits lead to excessive carried interest, subsequent losses trigger clawbacks. The distribution waterfall, a structured sequence, dictates the order in which profits are distributed among stakeholders. It ensures alignment of interests between general and limited partners.

**Critical Events Influencing Fund Dynamics**

*Key Person Events:* Key person events add a layer of risk management. If a key individual departs or is unable to fulfill responsibilities, protective measures, such as suspension of new investments, may be activated. The fund's agreement often includes provisions for LPs to vote on fund continuation in such scenarios.

Understanding the private equity timeline is paramount for investors and fund managers alike. The journey, marked by distinct phases and mechanisms, demands strategic planning, risk mitigation, and a commitment to long-term value creation. As funds navigate the complexities, the interplay of holding periods, vintage dynamics, and key mechanisms shapes the ultimate success of a private equity venture.

# Private Equity Economics

## Valuation in Private Equity

Valuing private companies in the context of Private Equity involves addressing specific challenges.

**Net Asset Value (NAV)**

Net Asset Value represents the fair value of a fund's assets, considering the market value of its investments and any outstanding liabilities. It serves as a key metric for assessing the overall health and performance of a Private Equity fund.

**Illiquidity Premium**

The illiquidity of private investments is a critical consideration. Investors often apply an illiquidity premium to account for the lack of market liquidity, reflecting the notion that illiquid investments should offer a higher return.

**Valuation Methods**

Private Equity valuation relies on multiple methods, with the Discounted Cash Flow (DCF) analysis being a prevalent approach. Additionally, Transaction Comparables and Public Company Comparables are employed to benchmark a company's valuation against industry peers.

# Fees and the J-Curve

Investors participating in Private Equity encounter specific fee structures and a phenomenon known as the J-curve.

**Fees**

Private Equity funds charge fees to cover operational and management expenses. Management fees are typically calculated as a percentage of committed capital. In addition to management fees, General Partners receive carried interest—a share of the profits once the fund surpasses the hurdle rate.

**The J-Curve**

The J-curve illustrates the typical pattern of returns in Private Equity. Initial returns may be negative as capital is deployed and investments are in their early stages. Over time, as portfolio companies mature and generate returns, the curve rises, ultimately yielding positive returns.

# Risks in Private Equity

While Private Equity offers numerous advantages, investors must navigate inherent risks associated with the asset class.

**Equity Risk**

Equity risk in Private Equity relates to exposure to market fluctuations and economic conditions. The success of portfolio companies is influenced by broader economic trends and industry-specific factors.

**Liquidity Risk**

Liquidity risk is a key consideration in Private Equity. Investments in private companies are illiquid, and exiting these investments can be challenging. This lack of liquidity may limit an investor's ability to swiftly liquidate holdings.

# New Trends in Private Equity

The landscape of Private Equity is continually evolving, with several trends reshaping the industry.

### The Democratization of Private Equity

Private Equity, once reserved for institutional investors and high-net-worth individuals, is becoming more accessible to the broader market. This trend, known as the democratization of Private Equity, is driven by the emergence of public Private Equity firms, Exchange-Traded Funds (ETFs), and Mutual Funds that provide retail investors with access to this asset class.

### Public Private Equity Firms

Several Private Equity firms have transitioned to become publicly traded entities. This move enhances transparency, provides liquidity for existing stakeholders, and opens avenues for retail investors to participate in the success of these firms.

### ETFs and Mutual Funds

These investment vehicles offer diversification benefits and allow investors to participate in a pool of private equity assets without directly owning individual companies. ETFs and Mutual Funds bring liquidity to a traditionally illiquid market, offering a more flexible and accessible entry point for a broader range of investors.

### Technology-Driven Innovations

The integration of technology is transforming the Private Equity landscape. Fintech solutions, data analytics, and artificial intelligence are being increasingly utilized for deal sourcing, due diligence, and performance monitoring. Technology-driven innovations enhance operational efficiency, provide deeper insights, and contribute to more informed decision-making.

**Sustainable and Impact Investing**

There is a growing emphasis on sustainable and impact investing within the Private Equity sphere. Investors are increasingly prioritizing Environmental, Social, and Governance (ESG) considerations, aligning their investments with ethical and sustainable practices. Private Equity firms are incorporating ESG criteria into their investment strategies, reflecting a broader societal shift towards responsible and purpose-driven capitalism.

# Global Private Equity AUM

### AUM Growth and Allocation

The global Assets Under Management (AUM) in Private Equity have witnessed significant growth, underlining its increasing prominence in the investment landscape. Private Equity's share of institutional portfolios has expanded, reflecting its appeal to investors seeking higher returns and portfolio diversification.

### Comparison to Other Asset Classes

When comparing Private Equity to other asset classes, such as public equities, fixed income, and real estate, it's essential to consider risk-return profiles, volatility, and correlation. Private Equity's unique characteristics, including illiquidity and active management, contribute to its distinct role in a well-balanced investment portfolio.

### Conclusion

In conclusion, Private Equity remains a compelling and evolving asset class that continues to attract investors seeking not only superior returns but also active involvement in the companies they invest in. With its diverse investment strategies, structured processes, and ongoing innovations, Private Equity offers a dynamic and flexible approach to value creation.

Investors venturing into Private Equity should be equipped with a comprehensive understanding of its nuances, including fund structures, valuation methods, associated risks, and the impact of emerging trends. This primer serves as a starting point for investors to navigate the multifaceted world of Private Equity, emphasizing the importance of due diligence, strategic decision-making, and a long-term perspective.

# Demystifying Private Equity: Beyond the Acronym

Private Equity, often abbreviated as PE, may appear as a complex and sophisticated investment realm, but at its core, it embodies the essence of PEOPLE and ENTREPRENEURSHIP. Here, I aim to provide a different perspective on certain aspects of PE, striving to be objective and fair to the average Joe and Jane who could wonder about the increasing gap between Average Doe and PE Dough!

### A Numbers Game: Money!

Regardless of the PE name, it is all about the money – and in a positive sense. The main driver for all PE activities is Money. There is no reason whatsoever for any person or entity to push their mortal limits to the extent PE requires except for financial gains – for all stakeholders.

### The Fundamental Investment

PE is not just an acronym; it's the essence of investment itself. All investments, at their inception, share the DNA of private equity. It is a Primal Form of Investment that has well evolved, primitive no more!

### An Endless Conflict between the Agent and the Principal

While it may be taken as a fact that PE General Partners operate as principals, that is far from reality. PE is a delicate balance where the General Partner dons the hats of both Agent and Principal. The Carried Interest and alignment on financial upside interest push the GP into the Principal (driver) seat, yet they remain Agents (Passengers) in one form or another. This duality introduces costs and risks, emphasizing the inherent agency dilemma in PE. I would say the highest cost and risk investors in PE funds incur is THE AGENCY COST.

## Reputation: The Currency of PE

In the world of PE, reputation is paramount. This is not utopic or normative; this is a basic expectation by all stakeholders. PE professionals operate in a realm where trust and credibility are currency. While missing unrealized gains might be forgiven, any compromise on integrity is unforgivable. This underscores the necessity of operating PE as a black box, not just by design but for the convenience of safeguarding the plural reputation of PE players. As the saying goes, "What happens in Vegas," PE professionals have been to this metaphoric Vegas many times and know one another very well.

## Private Equity, a Private Affair

This brings us to the heightened level of confidentiality (legal checks and balances) and discretion (disclosure on a need to know basis) PE operates in. It is often shrouded in secrecy, creating an enigma that intrigues professionals from various domains. Individuals from consulting, legal, corporate, accounting, and more aspire to understand the elusive nature of PE. Some would like to crack the code from OUT to IN and get frustrated by its high Chinese Walls.

## The Matrix: Blue or Red Pill?

PE is not just a functional expertise; it's a mindset, and given it is by no means a typical 9 to 5 job; it happens to be a lifestyle. PE professionals are akin to generalists aspiring to be specialists in numerous areas, expanding the matrix of industry and function. They want to morph somehow into supermen (and women). This is very demanding, and while they are too busy seeking transformation and substantial upside, they sometimes have those reflective moments and end up wondering if they made the right choice taking this path. This, and "easy money" Crypto happened!

## Mind the GAAP

Another interesting point is the tax haven status of PE investors, packaging profits as capital gains, this sparks continuous debate. It invites scrutiny and questions the fairness of this accounting practice (or planned exception). Even if this issue were addressed in any other format, it will only add a layer of complexity to the already intricate world of PE, where financial strategies often blur the lines between innovation and exploitation.

**Men in Black**

PE professionals are sometimes perceived as corporate "Men in Black," swooping in to restructure and beat down the weaker players. While some argue that PE-mandated restructuring is a strategic move and survival necessity, others see it as sugar-coating a deal for the subsequent buyer who will eventually deal with people! This dichotomy in perception reveals the contrasting realities that define PE in the eyes of different stakeholders.

**My Hockey Stick is Bigger (than yours)!"**

The term "Hockey Stick" is a commonplace in the realm of Private Equity (PE). In simple terms, it represents an exaggerated projection of growth that tends to accelerate either during or after a sale event, aiming to maximize the business value through discounted cash flow calculations and, consequently, the sale price. Whether in the buying or selling phase, PE professionals conduct Due Diligence to validate these hockey sticks, and interestingly, they are experts at both creating and admiring them. The humorous aspect lies in the fact that, regardless of the transaction side (buy or sell), PE professionals seem to have an affinity for Hockey Sticks. It becomes intrinsic to their personalities and overconfidence. They genuinely believe that, after falling in love with a business or sector, their bright minds and expertise would be rendered meaningless if they couldn't cultivate even larger hockey sticks. If you were to ask any PE professional about their most significant mistake, a particularly articulate response might be, "my large hockey stick!"

**Forget the J-curve; Focus on the L-curve!"**

When delving into the costly mistakes made by PE professionals, a significant aspect to consider is the price of learning. It's essential to note that not all PE professionals are thoroughly acquainted with the mandates their funds are about to undertake when deploying dry powder. Fund teams often comprise a peculiar mix of seasoned veterans, trophy hires and enthusiastic converts. It's not uncommon for the veterans to be senior and preoccupied, while the extra-PE converts are brimming with motivation and greenness. The decision-making process in the Investment Committee, that bustling room where substantial decisions are forged, can sometimes morph into a "jury-like" setting reminiscent of "12 Angry Men." The ability to navigate this dynamic terrain becomes paramount; failure to do so could result in the fund paying the steep cost of a learning curve. Arguably, this L-curve proves to be far more financially burdensome than any J-curve, particularly during the initial 2-3 years of the fund. Learning here is not just about the specific mandate or industry targeted but also, and more so, about understanding one another and crafting an efficient work dynamic.

*PE is not just an investment asset class; it's a dynamic interplay of people, entrepreneurship, reputation, and financial intricacies. It remains a multifaceted domain where success hinges not only on financial acumen but also on integrity, adaptability, and the ability to navigate the complex web of perceptions surrounding this enigmatic industry.*

# The Strategic Role of Operational Value Creation in Private Equity

*Why is Operational Value Creation (OVC) crucial in the PE industry, and what is the relative impact of OVC/OP compared to Deal Teams or market conditions?*

Operational Value Creation (OVC) stands as a linchpin in the Private Equity (PE) industry, wielding a profound influence on the growth and prosperity of portfolio companies. This section scrutinizes the pivotal role of OVC, seeking to quantify its contribution in comparison to Deal Teams and market conditions.

## Importance of Operational Value Creation in PE

*Enhancing Performance Beyond Financial Engineering*

Private equity firms acknowledge the constraints of relying solely on financial engineering for returns. OVC becomes indispensable, involving proactive measures to optimize operational efficiency, curtail costs, and amplify revenue streams.

*Navigating Market Volatility and Uncertainty*

In the capricious landscape of market conditions, OVC emerges as a stabilizing force. PE firms fortified with robust OVC strategies exhibit adeptness in navigating uncertainties, mitigating risks, and capitalizing on opportunities during economic fluctuations.

# Quantifying the Contribution of OVC to PE Value

*The Share of OVC in Portfolio Company Value*

A quantitative scrutiny of PE-backed companies unveils the tangible impact of OVC. Approximating the percentage distribution of value within portfolio companies sheds light on the significance of operational enhancements.

*Table : Contribution to PE Value - OVC vs. Deal Teams vs. Market Conditions*

| Aspect of Value Contribution | Percentage Share Range |
|---|---|
| Operational Value Creation (OVC) | 30-50% |
| Deal Teams | 20-40% |
| Market Conditions | 10-30% |

*Case Studies Illustrating OVC Impact*

Delving into case studies offers qualitative insights into how OVC initiatives directly influenced the financial and operational performance of PE-backed companies.

The strategic importance of Operational Value Creation in the PE industry cannot be overstated. Beyond financial engineering, OVC functions as a dynamic lever for navigating market uncertainties and elevating overall portfolio company performance. While the percentage distribution in Table 1 is illustrative and may vary, it emphasizes the profound impact of OVC in comparison to other PE factors.

*Note: The percentages in the able are approximate and subject to variations based on industry, sectors, and individual PE firms.*

# PE Trivia of Numbers

*Did you know these, or some of these, numbers before?*

| Trivia | Description |
| --- | --- |
| **750,000,000** | Average Fund Size: Since 2023, the average private equity fund closing size is $750 million. |
| **250,000 to 25,000,000** | Minimum Investment Size: Typically, $25 million, though some funds accept as low as $250,000. Fintech Innovation has started to allow for lower investment sizes into PE funds. |
| **50,000,000** | Round Size (Late Stage): Late-stage rounds led by private equity firms or hedge funds are typically $50 million and above. |
| **3 to 5** | Investment Period : Typical Investment Period for a PE fund is 3 to 5 years (Deployment Period). |
| **10** | Life Span: Private Equity funds have an average term span of ten years (Life Cycle); this is more than the 6 to 7 years of a Hedge Fund. |
| **80-20** | Rule in Private Equity Returns: Profits are typically split 80% to Limited Partners (LPs) and 20% to General Partners (GPs). |
| **2 and 20** | Fee Structure - Common in hedge funds and some private equity funds, consisting of a 2% annual management fee and a 20% performance fee. |
| **8 and 20** | Carried Interest: A profit sharing process for PE GPs (with LPs); most common 8% as a Hurdle Rate and a 20% as Profit Pool Split (80-20 rule). |
| **115** | Rule of 115 (Tripling Investment): Estimates the years needed to triple an investment (115 divided by the expected rate of return). |
| **72** | Rule of 72 in Equity (Doubling Investment): Estimates the number of years for an investment to double (72 divided by the expected rate of return). Ditto for 69, 70. |
| **8%** | The 8% Rule in Finance: Designed for higher returns with a safe withdrawal rate of 8%. |
| **20%** | 20% Rule in Shares (Nasdaq 20% Rule) : Requires stockholder approval before issuing 20% or more of outstanding common stock or voting power (US and Other Jurisdictions). |

**2040 Prediction:**

*While we all would agree that the $ numbers shall increase due to inflation, I would argue that the hurdle rate % and profit-split % of 8/20 respectively would also increase. As PE becomes more accessible to the average investor due to technology, there will be more PE firms willing to accept the challenge and for a higher threshold as a departure from the traditional big names. Also Investors will be willing to share a higher percentage of profit to make it worthwhile and more sustainable to the new PE GP/LP models.*

*For the same reasons above, the placement and management fees shall be under pressure and fall below the 2.5/2% marks.*

# PART 2 :

# A Primer on The Operating Partner in the PE World

# The Economics of Operational Partnerships in Private Equity

*"An OP to OVC is like bee to honey."*

## Operating Partner – The Honey Bee of Pee Eee!

Navigating the intricate world of private equity, the relationship between an Operating Partner (OP) and Operational Value Creation (OVC) can be likened to the magical dance of a bee and honey. Just as a bee diligently seeks out nectar to craft golden sweetness, an Operating Partner diligently strives to uncover and unlock the latent potential within portfolio companies, creating a metaphorical 'nectar' of value. The bee, with its precision and purpose, transforms raw nectar into liquid gold – a process mirroring the OP's role in converting latent opportunities into tangible, sustainable value. Much like the bee's vital contribution to the pollination cycle, an Operating Partner plays a crucial role in fertilizing the growth of portfolio companies. With a keen understanding of industry nuances, market dynamics, and operational intricacies, the OP becomes a catalyst, pollinating the business environment with strategic insights, innovation, and operational excellence. The sweetness of honey is not merely a result of the bee's efforts but a collective outcome of the intricate dance between the bee and the blossoms it selects on its seemingly random path. Similarly, the value created by an Operating Partner is not a solitary achievement but a collaboration between their expertise and the unique challenges and opportunities embedded in each portfolio company, and the way they decide to prioritize these opportunities. The bee seeks out the finest blooms for its nectar, much like an OP strategically identifies and nurtures the most promising buckets of value creation within their purview. Another parallel, is the total independence an OP must demonstrate when in the field, just like bees they are on their own and make their own decisions most of the times. This analogy extends further, as the bee's dance contributes to the broader ecosystem's vitality – a parallel to how an Operating Partner's efforts resonate beyond individual companies, influencing the overall health of the private equity landscape. Just as bees are essential to the vitality of nature, Operating Partners are integral to the thriving success of private equity investments. The interdependent relationship between an OP and the PE OVC, where diligence, precision, and purpose converge to produce a sweet, enduring impact on the portfolio companies they touch.

# Costs Associated with Operating Partners

*Are Operating Partners in Private Equity Clearly at a Better "Cost to Value"?*

Operating Partners (OPs) are not inexpensive by any means.

Assessing the value Operating Partners (OPs) offer to Private Equity (PE) companies requires an understanding of their cost dynamics. This section explores the usual costs of operating principals (OPs) and examines how these costs relate to the value produced. These costs include both monetary remuneration and upside incentives. The private equity company anticipates that returns from OVC targets will offset multiples of these expenditures.

| Compensation Component | Description |
|---|---|
| *Fixed Compensation* | *Typically includes base salaries and benefits, providing a stable income for the Operating Partner (OP).* |
| *Variable Performance-Based Bonuses* | *Linked to predefined performance metrics, these bonuses serve as incentives for outstanding contributions to portfolio company success.* |
| *Equity Participation* | *Represents a significant share of OP compensation, aligning their interests with the long-term success and value creation of portfolio companies.* |

# Value Contribution and Return on Investment

*Operational Efficiency and Value Creation:* OPs play a pivotal role in enhancing operational efficiency within portfolio companies. Their hands-on approach often results in streamlined processes, cost savings, and revenue growth, directly impacting the bottom line.

*Risk Mitigation and Problem Solving:* The ability of OPs to navigate challenges and mitigate risks contributes significantly to the resilience of portfolio companies. This proactive problem-solving approach adds intrinsic value to the PE firm.

*Strategic Guidance and Decision-Making:* Beyond day-to-day operations, OPs provide strategic guidance and contribute to critical decision-making. Their wealth of industry knowledge and operational expertise adds strategic depth to the PE firm's decision processes.

## Assessment of Cost-to-Value Ratio

*Balancing Cost and Value:* While the costs associated with OPs may seem substantial, the value they bring in terms of operational enhancements, risk mitigation, and strategic contributions often outweigh these expenses. The cost-to-value ratio becomes a pivotal metric in evaluating the efficiency of OP engagements.

*Upside Incentives and Alignment:* The inclusion of upside incentives, such as performance-based bonuses and equity participation, ensures a strong alignment of interests. This alignment is instrumental in fostering a collaborative environment where OPs are motivated to contribute to the sustained success of portfolio companies.

The economics of Operational Partnerships in Private Equity involve a strategic balance between costs and the value generated by OPs. The inclusion of fixed compensation, variable bonuses, and equity participation ensures a holistic approach to aligning OP interests with the success of portfolio companies. The value brought by OPs, both in immediate operational improvements and long-term strategic contributions, positions them as invaluable assets in the PE value creation process.

# The PE Factor:  OP as a Profit Center Amplifier

## Intricacies of OP Compensation

When examining Operating Partner (OP) compensation within Private Equity (PE), it's crucial to appreciate the nuanced interplay between fixed and variable components. The increment in fixed costs attributed to the OP's fixed compensation is a fraction of their total pay, especially considering the potential upside they bring. In a break from conventional cost-plus models, PE firms embrace a non-linear compensation structure, where variable components like Merit Bonuses and Equity Participation outweigh fixed elements, serving as rewards for outstanding performance and aligning OP interests with portfolio success.

## PE as the Amplifier of Upside Business

Adding complexity to this structure is the reliance on Carried Interest in the PE industry. Triggered above a specified hurdle rate, usually around 8%, Carried Interest links OP compensation directly to the fund's overall performance, transforming the paradigm into a performance-driven model where value accretion extends beyond incremental benefits. Leveraging strategies further contribute to this non-linearity, with the cost of debt often lower than the target internal rate of return (IRR). This financial engineering positions PE firms to extract additional value, creating a scenario where costs incurred by the OP for value creation are overshadowed by potential returns.

## Saving on OpCo C-Suite Shuffles

A compelling facet of OP involvement lies in their ability to augment acquired business CEOs. In cases of inherited or temporary CEOs, particularly in majority acquisitions from owner-founders, active OPs play a vital role in supporting and shadowing the incumbent CEO. This collaborative approach ensures a seamless transition, fostering stability and strategic guidance until a definitive leadership reshuffle is executed.

## Underinvesting in OP Resources: The Ultimate PE FOMO

Underinvesting in OP resources can be the ultimate PE FOMO. Paying less to an average-performing value creation lead translates to missing out on the most potent contribution lever into total returns. While trading off PE management fees (typically 2.5% of deployed capital equity), PE firms risk forgoing a much larger chunk of value – 20% of the upside above 8% on a significantly larger pool of leveraged investments exceeding 2x.

## ROI of High-Caliber OPs

In numerous cases, renowned PE firms view hiring a high-caliber OP as a 10-15x return on investment, emphasizing the pivotal role OPs play in enhancing the overall performance and success of portfolio companies.

# Performance Gaps in Private Equity: Impact of Active Operational Partners

*What are the performance gaps, measured in terms of Cash Multiples or IRR, between PE firms with active Operational Partners (OP) resources and those without, considering varied OP structures such as in-house or interim?*

The performance differentials within the Private Equity (PE) landscape are closely tied to the presence and nature of Operational Partners (OP). This section investigates the observable performance gaps, specifically in terms of Cash Multiples or Internal Rate of Return (IRR), between PE firms that harness active OP resources and those that do not, accounting for diverse OP structures.

## Performance Gaps in Private Equity

*Elevated Returns with Active Operational Partners* PE firms that strategically integrate active OP resources often outperform their counterparts. The synergies derived from OP involvement extend beyond financial engineering, leading to enhanced operational efficiency, risk mitigation, and value creation.

*Influence of Operational Partner Structures* The structure of OP engagement varies, encompassing in-house teams, interim appointments, or external partnerships. Understanding how different OP structures impact performance is vital for evaluating the effectiveness of OP contributions.

## Quantifying Performance Gaps

*Cash Multiples and IRR Comparison* Analyzing performance metrics, such as Cash Multiples and IRR, provides a quantitative lens to discern the impact of active OP involvement. The following table illustrates the

**40**

observed performance gaps between PE firms with and without active OP resources.

*Table : Performance Gaps - Active OP vs. Non Active OP*

| Performance Metric | Active OP Firms Range | Non Active OP Firms Range |
|---|---|---|
| Cash Multiples | 1.2-1.5x | 0.8-1.2x |
| Internal Rate of Return | 20-25% | 10-15% |

It is evident, when hiring the right OP, whatever cost structure they demand shall be overshadowed by the larger 0.3-0.4x additional Cash-on Cash or incremental 5-10% IRR.

# Additional Value Brought by Active OPs

| Additional Value Dimension | Active OP Firms Range |
|---|---|
| Talent Development | High |
| Risk Mitigation | Proactive |
| Strategic Alignment | Coherent |
| Non-Financial Metrics | Positive Trends |

The presence of active Operational Partners emerges as a decisive factor in driving superior performance within the Private Equity sector. The observed performance gaps, whether measured in Cash Multiples or IRR, accentuate the strategic advantage afforded by effective OP engagement, underscoring the value of operational expertise in amplifying returns.

# Models for Operating Value Creation (OVC

## Operational Partner (OP) Management Model in Private Equity

Private Equity (PE) firms employ diverse models to drive Operating Value Creation (OVC) and manage Operational Partners (OPs), tailoring approaches to meet the unique needs of each portfolio company.

| Model | Description | Advantages | Disadvantages |
|---|---|---|---|
| **In-House Operating Partners** | Cultivation of an in-house team of OPs, collaborating closely with deal teams and portfolio companies for operational enhancements. | Direct integration, deep understanding of firm strategies. | Limited external perspectives, potential for insularity. |
| **External Consulting Partnerships** | Engagement of external consultants or specialized firms for project-specific or portfolio-wide operational expertise. | Access to specialized knowledge, flexibility in resource allocation. | Reliance on external expertise, potential higher costs for premium consulting services. |

| | | | |
|---|---|---|---|
| **Interim or Part-Time OPs** | Hiring OPs on an interim or part-time basis for specific projects or critical phases of a portfolio company's development. | Cost-effectiveness, flexibility in leveraging expertise. | Potential lack of long-term commitment, challenges in building sustained relationships. |
| **Strategic Partnerships with Industry Experts** | Formation of strategic partnerships with industry experts or executives acting as advisors or mentors. | Access to industry-specific insights, leveraging external networks. | Limited availability of industry experts, potential conflicts of interest. |
| **Portfolio Operations Teams** | Establishment of dedicated Portfolio Operations Teams to drive operational improvements across the entire portfolio. | Centralized oversight, consistent approach to OVC. | Potential coordination challenges, resource allocation conflicts. |
| **Specialized Operating Partnerships (SOPs)** | Formation of specialized operating partnerships with industry experts contributing to multiple portfolio companies. | Cross-pollination of expertise, shared insights, and best practices. | Potential resource allocation challenges, varying levels of commitment from SOPs. |
| **Technology-Driven OVC** | Integration of data analytics, AI, and automation tools as part of the OVC strategy. | Enhanced efficiency, scalability through technology-driven solutions. | High initial implementation costs, potential resistance to technological changes. |

These models are often used in combination, allowing PE firms to create customized operational strategies based on the specific requirements of

**43**

their portfolio companies. The evolving landscape of PE operations continually shapes and refines these models to maximize value creation.

# PE Lifecycle and Stage Coverage by the OP

## Deciphering the Diverse Involvement by Stage Models of Operational Partners in Private Equity

In the complex landscape of Private Equity (PE), Operational Partners (OPs) play a multifaceted role that extends beyond the post-deal phase. Contrary to common perceptions, OPs contribute value across the entire deal continuum, from pre-deal evaluations to the detailed execution of post-deal strategies. As the PE industry evolves, so do the models of OP involvement, presenting a range of approaches customized to meet the specific needs of each portfolio company. This exploration delves into four distinct OP Involvement Models, shedding light on how these strategic experts navigate their impact, whether at the forefront of pre-deal planning or seamlessly integrated into the intricacies of post-deal operations. Join us on a journey through the operational landscape, where OPs emerge not just as partners but as crucial contributors to comprehensive and forward-thinking value creation.

| Model by Stage | Description | Advantages | Disadvantages | Activity |
|---|---|---|---|---|
| **Post-Deal Only (Traditional Model)** | OP involvement begins after the deal is closed, focusing on optimizing operational efficiency and driving value in the post-acquisition phase. | Deep dive into existing operations, targeted improvements based on acquired insight. | Limited influence on deal sourcing and evaluation, potential missed opportunities in shaping pre-deal strategies. | 100-Day Planning, Monitoring, NED/Advisory, Value Creation/Turnaround, Functional Advisory, Exit Readiness |
| **Pre-Deal Only (Front-Loaded Model)** | OPs are engaged in the pre-deal phase, working closely with deal | Early identification of operational challenges and | Reduced focus on post-deal execution, potential | Deal Sourcing, Due Diligence, Investment Strategy/Thesis, |

| | | | | |
|---|---|---|---|---|
| | teams to assess potential targets, identify operational risks and opportunities, and inform the overall deal strategy. | opportunities, proactive integration of operational due diligence. | misalignment between pre-deal assessments and post-deal operational strategies. | Management Assessment, Transaction Execution |
| **Continuous Involvement (Integrated Model)** | OPs are involved throughout the deal lifecycle, from pre-deal assessment to post-deal execution and ongoing value creation. This model emphasizes seamless collaboration between deal teams and OPs to drive holistic value. | Comprehensive alignment of operational insights with deal strategies, continuous optimization. | Requires strong coordination between deal teams and OPs, potential resource challenges in maintaining continuous involvement. | Deal Sourcing, Due Diligence, Investment Strategy/Thesis, Management Assessment, Transaction Execution, 100-Day Planning, Monitoring, NED/Advisory, Value Creation/Turnaround, Functional Advisory, Exit Readiness |
| **Flexible Engagement (Adaptive Model)** | OP involvement is adapted based on the unique needs of each deal. Depending on deal characteristics, OPs may focus more on either pre-deal or post-deal activities or switch between the two as required. | Tailored approach based on deal-specific requirements, flexibility in resource allocation. | Potential challenges in determining the optimal level of OP involvement for each deal, risk of inconsistency in approach. | Activity allocation depends on deal-specific requirements and may vary between deal phases. |

These OVC/OP Involvement Models reflect the evolving nature of PE operational strategies, highlighting the importance of considering operational expertise at every stage of the deal lifecycle. The choice of a particular model depends on the specific requirements of each deal and the overall PE firm strategy.

# OP Excellence

## Other Scenarios and Specialties where OPs Rise, Shine and Soar

OPs are not just meant to be leaders of traditional OVC process, but rather key players across a wide range of specialty situational operating theaters and modes: Board Representation, Turnaround, Restructuring, Regional Up-Scaling, etc.

## OPs Make Excellent Board Members!

PE firms have to make key decisions early on when an investment is made, who will be their representative on the NewCo board. Their deal teams could be extremely busy or not adept to the desired challenge, and their network of independent advisors might not be totally aligned on certain intricacies this role brings about. Here the OP stands as ideal candidate; in fact, being on the board makes their mandate easier to fulfill.

**Strategic Board Impact: The Crucial Role of PE-Appointed Operational Partners (OPs)**

In the Private Equity (PE) landscape, appointing Operational Partners (OPs) to board positions brings distinctive advantages that extend beyond direct operational influence. Here are three major points highlighting the significant benefits:

**1. Operational Pragmatism in Strategic Decision-Making:**

- *Operational Expertise Meets Strategic Vision:* PE-appointed OPs infuse board discussions with a pragmatic operational perspective. This ensures that strategic decisions align not just with financial goals but are also attuned to the practicalities and challenges faced at the operational level.

## 2. Bridging the Strategy-Execution Gap:

- *Seamless Alignment of Strategy and Operations:* OPs, with their deep operational understanding, act as a bridge between high-level strategic decisions and on-the-ground execution. This alignment ensures that board strategies are not just conceptual but are effectively implementable, reducing the gap between vision and execution.

## 3. Proactive Risk Management and Continuity:

- *Mitigating Risks with Operational Insights:* PE-appointed OPs contribute to proactive risk management at the board level. Their ability to foresee operational challenges enhances the board's capability to identify and mitigate risks effectively. Additionally, in times of leadership transitions, OPs offer stability by seamlessly stepping into interim roles, ensuring continuity in strategic direction.

# Unlocking Value in Crisis: An Obvious Case for OPs

When an Operating Company is in crisis, such as low cash balance, breached covenants, losing sales below its economies of scale sweet spot, etc., calling in an Operating Partner as Mr./Ms. Fix It is a welcome and no-surprise decision.

**The Pivotal Role of Operational Value Creation (OVC) and Operational Partners (OPs) in Private Equity Restructuring and Turnaround Strategies**

In the dynamic realm of Private Equity (PE), there are moments when the traditional rulebook takes a backseat, and a more robust, even radical, approach is warranted. This typically unfolds in scenarios demanding a major corporate restructuring or a complete turnaround. The strategic deployment of Operational Value Creation (OVC) initiatives, often spearheaded by Operational Partners (OPs), becomes not merely beneficial but paramount during these critical phases. Let's delve into the heightened significance of OVC and OPs in the context of PE firms navigating the complexities of restructuring and turnaround.

1. **Diagnostic Precision in Crisis:**

   - **Unveiling Underlying Issues:** Amidst a restructuring or turnaround, the ability to diagnose and fathom the root causes of underperformance is paramount. OPs, armed with an in-depth understanding of operations, engage in meticulous diagnostics, unraveling hidden inefficiencies, operational bottlenecks, and areas demanding immediate intervention.

2. **Swift and Decisive Action:**

   - **Operational Agility:** Turnaround situations demand nimbleness. OPs bring operational agility to the forefront, promptly identifying areas for immediate action. Their hands-on involvement ensures

**49**

that decisions are made promptly, steering the portfolio company away from further distress.

### 3. Rigorous OVC Strategies:

- **Comprehensive Turnaround Plans:** OVC takes center stage with the formulation of rigorous turnaround plans. OPs collaborate with existing management to implement operational improvements, cost-saving measures, and revenue enhancement strategies. The goal is not just recovery but a sustainable metamorphosis.

### 4. Hands-On Execution:

- **Immediate Hands-On Involvement:** OPs actively participate in the execution of the formulated strategies. Whether it's restructuring internal processes, optimizing the supply chain, or implementing lean practices, their hands-on involvement accelerates the pace of change, a critical element in turnaround scenarios.

### 5. Crisis Management and Stabilization:

- **Navigating Financial Distress:** Operational Partners adeptly navigate financial distress, employing strategies to stabilize the financial health of the portfolio company. This includes renegotiating contracts, managing cash flow, and identifying opportunities for quick wins to boost liquidity.

### 6. Leadership Augmentation:

- **Leadership Reinforcement:** In situations where leadership gaps contribute to the crisis, OPs often step into interim leadership roles. This ensures stability, strategic direction, and immediate action while the firm identifies a long-term leadership solution.

### 7. Strategic Pivot and Innovation:

- **Pivoting Business Models:** OVC strategies, guided by OP expertise, may involve a strategic pivot in the business model. This could mean entering new markets, diversifying product lines, or embracing innovative approaches to meet market demands.

## 8. Alignment with Stakeholder Expectations:

- **Communication and Transparency:** OVC, led by OPs, places a premium on transparent communication. Managing stakeholder expectations becomes a critical aspect, and OPs play a pivotal role in aligning communication with the strategic narrative of the turnaround.

## 9. Flexibility in Resource Allocation:

- **Resource Optimization:** OPs bring a flexible approach to resource allocation. In a turnaround, where resource optimization is paramount, their ability to channel resources to high-impact areas is a decisive factor in the success of OVC initiatives.

## 10. Post-Turnaround Value Creation:

- **Sustainable Value Beyond Recovery:** OVC strategies extend beyond crisis resolution. OPs work towards sustainable value creation, ensuring that the operational improvements implemented during the turnaround phase become ingrained in the company's culture for long-term success.

In essence, during periods of major restructuring or turnaround, OVC guided by Operational Partners becomes not just a value-add but a critical lifeline for portfolio companies facing distress. The amalgamation of diagnostic precision, swift action, rigorous strategies, and hands-on execution positions OVC as the catalyst for not just recovery but a reinvigorated and resilient future. As an integral part of PE and portfolio company dynamics, OVC and OPs emerge as the strategic fresh-look "leave your ego at the door" solution, guiding the transformational steps towards a brighter, more sustainable outcome.

# Regionally Tailored OVC Strategies

In a fast-changing landscape of global business, Operational Value Creation (OVC) strategies exhibit nuanced variations across regions, necessitating a keen understanding for effective implementation by Private Equity (PE) firms. Crafting OVC strategies that align with the unique characteristics of each global landscape is paramount. This regional tailoring emphasizes the need for Operational Partners (OPs) who can act as functional experts and regional champions simultaneously.

**The Role of the OP as Regional Champions**

### 1. Cultural Work Styles:

- *Risk Appetite and Innovation:* Diverse cultural work styles impact how businesses operate. Some regions exhibit a penchant for risk-taking and innovation, while others adhere to more conservative approaches. Recognizing these cultural nuances is pivotal for PE firms crafting OVC strategies tailored to each locale.

### 2. Regulatory Game Plan:

- *Strategic Compliance:* Every jurisdiction introduces a set of regulatory rules akin to a strategic game. Navigating this regulatory landscape strategically is imperative for PE firms, akin to mastering a game. Adherence to rules varies globally, influencing the design and execution of OVC strategies.

### 3. Market Dynamics:

- *Riding Economic Waves:* Global markets are dynamic, resembling either a rollercoaster or a merry-go-round. Some markets exhibit volatile swings, while others maintain a steadier pace. Understanding these market dynamics allows PE firms to calibrate OVC strategies in alignment with the economic temperament of each region.

**4. Financial Landscape:**

- *Managing Economic Fluctuations:* Financial scenarios resemble a rollercoaster ride, characterized by peaks and troughs. PE firms must adeptly navigate these fluctuations, tailoring financial strategies to the economic undulations of each region. What proves effective in one economic landscape may require adaptation in another.

**5. Tech Adoption Spectrum:**

- *Strategic Tech Deployment:* Technology preferences differ globally, ranging from cutting-edge innovation to fundamental tools. PE firms should gauge the tech-savviness of each region, adopting a strategic approach in deploying technology. It's akin to selecting the appropriate tools, whether a state-of-the-art smartphone or a conventional flip phone.

This comprehensive approach to OVC recognizes that OPs play a dual role as functional experts and regional champions. Their ability to navigate cultural, regulatory, and market nuances makes them invaluable in tailoring OVC strategies for optimal impact across diverse global landscapes.

# Navigating Industry-Specific OVC Challenges

Understanding the intricacies of Operational Value Creation (OVC) in various industries is paramount for Private Equity (PE) firms. Recognizing the unique challenges and opportunities each sector presents, Operational Partners (OPs) act as functional experts, addressing industry-specific nuances to optimize value creation.

## The Role of the OP as a Functional Expert

| Industry Sector | Challenges & Opportunities | OP's Functional Expertise |
|---|---|---|
| **Manufacturing Sector** | *Supply Chain Optimization:* Efficiency and Cost Reduction | *Functional Expertise:* Supply Chain Dynamics Optimization |
| **Technology and Innovation** | *Rapid Tech Evolution:* Staying Competitive in Dynamic Tech Landscape | *Functional Expertise:* Cutting-edge Tech Innovations |
| **Healthcare Industry** | *Regulatory Compliance:* Navigating Stringent Regulations | *Functional Expertise:* Regulatory Compliance Navigation |
| **Consumer Goods and Retail** | *Market Trends and Consumer Behavior:* Adapting to Evolving Preferences | *Functional Expertise:* Trend Analysis, Consumer Behavior Understanding |
| **Energy and Utilities** | *Sustainability Integration:* Balancing Efficiency with Environmental Responsibility | *Functional Expertise:* Sustainability Practices Guidance |
| **Financial Services** | *Regulatory Changes:* Adapting to Shifting Financial Regulations | *Functional Expertise:* Financial Regulatory Dynamics |
| **Real Estate Development** | *Market Volatility:* Navigating Fluctuations in Real Estate Markets | *Functional Expertise:* Real Estate Market Dynamics |

# Strategic Management of Operational Partners (OPs) in Private Equity

**Precision in Hiring, Resilience in Retention**

Balancing precision in hiring with strategies for continuous engagement and growth enhances operational excellence in the PE landscape. In harmonizing OP management, these approaches enable PE firms to attract top-tier talent and foster enduring partnerships, contributing significantly to sustained success.

## Precision in Talent Acquisition Strategies

**1.1 Strategic Skill Set Definition:**

- Tailor recruitment strategies to specific skill sets.

- Align capabilities with diverse industry needs.

**1.2 Building Collaborative Networks:**

- Cultivate connections with executive search firms and industry associations.

- Establish long-term partnerships with OPs.

# Resilience in Retention Strategies

**2.1 Performance-Linked Incentives:**

- Link OP compensation to overall portfolio success.

- Recognize contributions and support career development.

**2.2 Continuous Engagement and Feedback:**

- Implement transparent evaluation systems.

- Provide continuous learning opportunities.

# Education and Qualifications for Operating Partners

### A Diverse Landscape of Expertise

Operating Partners come from diverse educational backgrounds, and while there is no set template for academic qualifications, there are a few common educational paths and degrees seen among operating partners. The specific discipline or certifications held may vary depending on the industry focus or individual expertise.

Common academic education for operating partners includes:

1. Business Administration: A degree in Business Administration, such as a Bachelor's or Master's in Business Administration (MBA), is a common qualification for operating partners. This degree provides a broad understanding of various business functions, including finance, strategy, operations, and leadership.

2. Finance or Economics: A degree in Finance or Economics provides a strong foundation in financial analysis, investment principles, and market dynamics. This knowledge is highly relevant to operating partners, as they often work closely with financial models, conduct due diligence, and assess investment opportunities.

3. Engineering or Technology: In industries such as technology, manufacturing, or engineering-focused sectors, operating partners may hold degrees in Engineering or related fields. This technical background allows them to bring specialized knowledge to optimize operations, assess technology investments, and drive innovation.

4. Industry-Specific Degrees: Depending on the industry focus of the private equity firm, operating partners may hold degrees specific to that industry. For example, a healthcare-focused private equity firm may have operating partners with degrees in Medicine or Healthcare Administration, while a renewable energy-focused firm may have operating partners with degrees in Environmental Science or Sustainable Energy.

In addition to academic education, operating partners may also hold certifications or specialized qualifications relevant to their industry or specific expertise. Some common certifications and qualifications for operating partners include:

1. Chartered Financial Analyst (CFA): The CFA designation is widely recognized in the finance and investment industry. It demonstrates expertise in areas such as financial analysis, investment valuation, and portfolio management.

2. Six Sigma: Operating partners involved in process improvement and operational efficiency may hold Six Sigma certifications. Six Sigma provides tools and techniques for eliminating defects and improving operational performance.

3. Professional certifications: Depending on the industry focus, operating partners may hold professional certifications relevant to their field. For example, in healthcare private equity, operating partners may hold certifications such as Certified Healthcare Executive (CHE) or Certified Healthcare Financial Professional (CHFP).

While academic education and certifications provide a solid foundation, it's important to note that experience, expertise, and a track record of successful value creation are often highly valued qualifications for operating partners.

Real-world experience and a deep understanding of specific industries or functional areas prove invaluable in driving operational excellence and creating value within portfolio companies.

# Operating Partner (OP) Compensation Structure

The compensation structure for Operating Partners (OPs) within the realm of private equity exhibits a degree of flexibility, with various factors influencing their remuneration. The nature of OP compensation is largely contingent on the terms outlined in individual agreements negotiated between the OP and the private equity (PE) firm. While there is a prevailing trend for OPs to receive compensation primarily from the PE fund, exceptions exist, and OPs may negotiate additional fees directly from portfolio companies (OpCos).

## Compensation from PE Fund

1. **Base Salary:** OPs commonly receive a base salary from the PE fund in recognition of their advisory services. This financial acknowledgment is designed to remunerate OPs for their time, expertise, and substantial contributions to the enhancement of portfolio companies.

2. **Carried Interest:** A pivotal component of OP compensation is often tied to carried interest. This structure aligns the interests of OPs with the overall success of the PE fund, as they are entitled to a share of the profits generated by the fund.

# Additional Compensation from OpCos

In certain scenarios, OPs may engage in separate negotiations to secure supplementary compensation directly from OpCos. This additional compensation can manifest in diverse forms such as consulting fees, director fees, or other arrangements, distinct from the compensation received from the PE fund.

In some case, OP can have an Equity Participation in the OpCo.

The intricacies of OP compensation, including the distribution between fund-level compensation and OpCo-derived compensation, are subject to negotiation. Collaborative discussions among OPs, PE funds, and OpCos contribute to the formulation of a compensation structure aligned with the unique goals, expertise, and impact that OPs bring to portfolio company performance.

It's imperative to recognize that the detailed terms of OP compensation are explicitly outlined in agreements between the OP and the PE fund. The considerable variability in these structures underscores the significance of individual circumstances and negotiation dynamics.

# OP Hiring and Reporting Structure

*Who Hires and Fires the OP?*

*To Whom does the OP report to?*

Beyond the realm of compensation, the role, and dynamics of Operating Partners (OPs) within private equity organizations are characterized by specific considerations related to their hiring, reporting lines, employment security, and capacity.

*Hiring Process:*

1. **Selection by PE Firms:** OPs are typically selected and hired by private equity (PE) firms. The criteria for selection may encompass the OP's industry expertise, operational experience, and a track record of success in driving value within portfolio companies.

2. **Alignment with Portfolio Needs:** The hiring decision is often driven by the PE firm's assessment of the specific needs and challenges faced by its portfolio companies. OPs are chosen based on their ability to address these needs and contribute to the overall success of the portfolio.

*Reporting Structure:*

1. **Direct Reporting to PE Leadership:** OPs commonly report directly to the leadership of the private equity firm. This reporting structure ensures a streamlined flow of communication and coordination between OPs and the decision-makers within the PE organization.

2. **Collaboration with Portfolio Company Leadership:** While OPs report to PE leadership, their role may involve close collaboration with the leadership teams of individual portfolio companies. This

collaborative approach aims to facilitate effective execution of value-creation strategies within the portfolio.

*Employment Dynamics:*

1. **Contractual Agreements:** The employment relationship between OPs and PE firms is governed by contractual agreements. These agreements outline the terms of engagement, including the duration of the relationship, performance expectations, and compensation details.

2. **Termination Clauses:** OP agreements may include provisions related to termination, specifying the circumstances under which the engagement can be terminated. This ensures clarity regarding the conditions that may lead to the conclusion of the OP's role within the organization.

*Executive or Advisory Capacity:*

1. **Varied Capacities:** OPs may operate in either executive or advisory capacities, depending on the specific needs of the PE firm and its portfolio companies. In an executive capacity, an OP may take on interim leadership roles within portfolio companies, driving operational changes. In an advisory capacity, the focus is often on providing strategic guidance and leveraging industry expertise.

2. **Flexibility in Roles:** The flexibility of OP roles allows PE firms to deploy these experts in a manner that maximizes their impact on portfolio company performance. Whether as interim executives, board members, or strategic advisors, OPs contribute to value creation based on the distinctive requirements of each situation.

The intricate interplay between Operating Partners, private equity firms, and portfolio companies underscores the dynamic nature of their collaboration. By navigating the complexities of hiring, reporting structures, employment dynamics, and varied capacities, OPs play a crucial role in driving operational excellence and fostering growth within the private equity ecosystem. Understanding the nuances of these relationships is essential for optimizing the contributions of OPs and maximizing the value they bring to portfolio companies.

**63**

# Operating Partners vs Deal Teams

## Navigating the Dynamic Relationship Between Operating Partners and Deal Teamers

*"Harmony in the Hustle House: Architects, Renovators and Flippers"*

*If the PE business was about house building, then Deal Teams are Architects (and Builders), and Operating Partners are Renovators. So Who are the Flippers: Flippers are those evolved PE players who figured out early on the essence of the PE game; they cracked the code per se. They learnt that Money (remember that little detail that drives the PE industry and the world) is the key target and will do the necessary and sufficient effort of designing, building and renovating to maximize the resale price.*

*One can argue that OPs, who come from Deal Team backgrounds, make excellent Flippers.*

*Below, we are going to shed light on how those architects, builders, renovators and flippers work together...*

# Operating Partners and Deal Teams: Convergence and Divergence Points

In the intricate landscape of private equity (PE) firms, the dynamics between Operating Partner (OP) or Operating Value Creation (OVC) teams and Deal teams play a pivotal role in steering the course of investments. The relationship is a delicate dance of convergence and divergence, where each team contributes distinct expertise to the overall success of the firm.

| Convergence Points: | Divergence Points: |
|---|---|
| Strategic Alignment: Both OP/OVC and Deal teams share the overarching goal of maximizing returns for the fund and its stakeholders. Strategic alignment occurs during investment decisions and the subsequent value creation phase. | Focus and Timeline: Deal teams are primarily involved in the identification, negotiation, and acquisition of investment opportunities. On the other hand, OP/OVC teams focus on operational improvements and long-term value creation post-acquisition. Divergence lies in the temporal aspects of their involvement. |
| Portfolio Company Success: Success for both teams is measured by the performance and growth of portfolio companies. Collaborative efforts are crucial in ensuring these companies meet their full potential. | Skill Set Emphasis: Deal teams excel in due diligence, financial modeling, and deal structuring. OP/OVC teams bring operational expertise, emphasizing efficiency, and strategic implementation. The divergence lies in the specialized skill sets each team possesses. |

# Power Dynamics:

| Deal Teams: | OP/OVC Teams: |
|---|---|
| Traditionally, deal teams wield significant influence during the deal sourcing and decision-making phases. Their power lies in identifying lucrative investment opportunities and securing favorable terms. | As the investment matures, the influence of OP/OVC teams rises. Their power is manifested in the ability to enhance operational efficiency, innovate strategies, and ultimately deliver on value creation promises. |

# Role Transitions help bridge the gap

- **Flexibility in Movement:** In dynamic PE environments, there's often fluidity in team member roles. Professionals may transition from deal-focused roles to operational roles and vice versa. This flexibility ensures a holistic understanding of the investment lifecycle and help improve the collaborative ecosystem.

**Key to Success:**

- **Effective Collaboration:** The success of a PE firm hinges on seamless collaboration between Deal teams and OP/OVC teams. Communication channels must remain open to bridge gaps between the deal-making vision and the operational reality.

- **Strategic Succession:** Strategic succession planning involves cultivating talent within the firm. This ensures a steady influx of professionals who understand both deal dynamics and operational intricacies.

In essence, the dynamic between OPs/OVCs and Deal teams is a symbiotic relationship that evolves across the investment timeline. The key to unlocking the full potential of a PE investment lies in recognizing the unique strengths each team brings to the table and fostering a collaborative ecosystem where the convergence and divergence points are orchestrated for maximum impact.

# Operating Partners vs CEOs

## Navigating the Complex Relationship Between Operating Partners and CEOs

"The Lady and The Tramp; ... and the Prima Donna"

*It's funny to compare the dynamic relationship between CEOs and Operating Partners (OPs) in the private equity space to 'The Lady and the Tramp,' but there's an unexpected twist: there could be a Prima Donna involved. It may be interesting to have a politically correct argument about who should do whatever function, but ultimately, it comes down to the individual preferences of the CEO and OP. Whichever metaphorical character is selected, it is important to remember the underlying warning: Don't turn into a Prima Donna. The focus is on avoiding an ego-driven attitude that might upset the delicate balance needed for a successful relationship in this complex dance of collaboration and conflict. Whether one imagines themself as the Prima Donna, the shrewd Tramp, or the elegant Lady, the essence lies in fostering a collaborative and value-driven relationship rather than succumbing to the pitfalls of ego-centric behavior.*

In more sophisticated terms, the partnership between CEOs and Operating Partners (OPs) in the private equity landscape is a nuanced   magnet spin that can oscillate between collaboration and tension. This intricate relationship forms the backbone of organizational decision-making, value creation, and strategic execution. This exploration will delve into the various facets of the CEO-OP dynamic, shedding light on the inherent challenges, underlying dynamics, and potential remedies that can pave the way for a much-needed harmonious collaboration.

## Unraveling the Tensions

*Understanding the Complexity:* Most CEOs have minimal experience navigating the dynamics of a relationship with an OP appointed by a PE firm or the board. The inherent mistrust, miscommunication, and competitive undercurrents can lead to a misalignment of objectives, diverting focus from the core agenda of value creation. To grasp the essence of this relationship, it's crucial to examine how CEOs perceive the role of the OP within the organizational hierarchy.

*The OP realm as a black box:* Studies have revealed disparities in perceptions between CEOs and OPs. For instance, when examining one dissatisfaction with another, a significant gap emerges – 39% of CEOs express dissatisfaction compared to the mere 3% anticipated by OPs. This disconnect underscores a fundamental issue: OPs might lack insight into how CEOs truly perceive their contributions and probably have done little effort to better explain their role and "good" intentions.

## The Value-Add Conundrum

*Defining Value Addition:* Around 70% of OPs believe they bring "significant value" to their work, contrasting sharply with the mere 20% of CEOs who share this sentiment (about the OP). Moreover, a notable 30% of CEOs believe OPs contribute only "little value," or worse, negative value. This stark misalignment in perceived contributions raises questions about the actual impact OPs have on organizational value creation.

*Cost/Benefit Evaluation:* The cost/benefit analysis further complicates matters. While approximately half of CEOs feel that OPs fall short in justifying their costs, a staggering ten times more OPs believe they bring 10x (the famous 10x+ ROI!) or more value compared to their costs. This disconnect highlights a substantial gap in understanding the tangible returns on investment in OPs.

## Navigating the Path Forward

*CEO Recommendations for Effectiveness:* CEOs offer insightful suggestions for OPs to enhance their effectiveness. Key recommendations include focusing on building trust, prioritizing value creation, and functioning as a resource to the CEO rather than aligning with the board. These recommendations underscore the need for a strategic shift in the approach of OPs to foster a more collaborative and impactful relationship.

*Creating a Foundation of Trust:* Companies with successful CEO-OP relationships emphasize the importance of trust. Open communication, confidentiality in discussions, and candid conversations about engagement rules are highlighted as essential components. These insights provide a roadmap for OPs to build a foundation of trust, fostering more effective collaboration.

*The OP Perspective:* OPs express the importance of collaboration and a partnership approach. Acknowledging the need for discretion in privileged conversations, OPs emphasize their commitment to creating equity value for mutual benefit.


The CEO-OP relationship is a dynamic interplay of expectations, perceptions, and collaborative efforts. Acknowledging the tensions, understanding the value-add conundrum, and embracing the path forward with trust and collaboration can redefine this relationship. As organizations strive for optimal performance and value creation, nurturing a symbiotic CEO-OP alliance emerges as a strategic imperative in the ever-evolving landscape of private equity-backed enterprises.

# The Operating Partner as Interim CEO

*"The Sky Diving OP: How to land safely as CEO"*

*The Sky Diving OP: How to land safely as a CEO" is akin to a cosmic adventure where some OpCo personnel might perceive the OP as an extraterrestrial being parachuted into their midst. It's like executing a daring 'behind enemy lines' drop, and the OP needs to hit the ground running, adjusting their behavior and jargon like a linguistic chameleon to seamlessly adapt to the OpCo's atmosphere. The higher the dive or steeper the challenge, the more acrobatic the process becomes. A colleague once quipped that most OPs operate like airplanes hovering at 3000 ft; too low, and they risk crashing into details (like choosing the canteen's menu!); too high, and they risk imploding with textbooks and theories (hello, Management by Objective MBO). Savvy OPs know how to change altitude. Nevertheless, when a PE firm tasks an OP to be an OpCo CEO, whether interim or otherwise, there's no other interpretation; they've been 'Skydived' and must now walk the talk, proving to the countless CEOs they've dealt with and mentored (at times, even fired!) that they can indeed don the CEO hat, not just talk about it. It's a celestial plunge into leadership, where failure is a dark abyss, and success means navigating all sorts of strange currents with finesse. One might argue that the role of the Interim CEO is quite the challenge, dwarfing even full-time CEO roles; in the former, they have to lead knowing that they come with an expiry date, and come midnight, their magic will only last if it made true sense to both the selfless and selfish.*

# The OPEO:  The Operating Partner Executive  Officer

Operating Partners (OPs) within the private equity landscape often play a pivotal role in managing transitions, providing stability, and driving strategic initiatives within portfolio companies. One significant facet of their engagement involves stepping into interim CEO or CXO positions, acting as a bridge during critical phases such as leadership transitions, business stabilization, or post-M&A integration.

## The Merits of Bridge Engagements: Interim and Fractional Roles

Operating Partners (OPs) serve as strategic linchpins during transitions within portfolio companies. Their engagements, especially in interim CEO or CXO roles, offer significant advantages in fostering stability, guiding strategic initiatives, and ensuring operational continuity. The multifaceted contributions of OPs during these bridge engagements are illuminated by industry insights.

1.  **Ensuring Operational Continuity:**

    - OPs act as stabilizing forces during turbulent periods within portfolio companies.

    - Strategic decision-making remains uninterrupted, contributing to sustained operational performance.

2.  **Facilitating Knowledge Transfer:**

    - Knowledge transfer to existing leadership teams enhances organizational resilience.

**72**

- OPs leverage their expertise to navigate complexities and share insights with the team.

3. **Strategic Contributions:**

   - OPs make strategic contributions to guide companies through transitions.

   - Their role extends beyond day-to-day operations, encompassing high-stakes decision-making.

# Varied Time Frames in Bridge Engagements

OP engagements in interim roles vary in duration, aligning with the specific needs and objectives of portfolio companies.

1. **Short-Term Engagements (3-6 Months):**

   - Address immediate needs and stabilize businesses during transitional phases.

2. **Medium-Term Engagements (6-12 Months):**

   - Oversee transformations or guide companies through critical growth stages.

3. **Long-Term Engagements (12+ Months):**

   - Serve in long-term interim roles, especially during complex integrations or leadership transitions.

# Ownership Transition and Post-M&A Scenarios

OPs play crucial roles in ownership transitions and post-M&A scenarios, contributing to the seamless continuation of operations and leadership alignment.

1. **Ownership Transition:**

   - OPs facilitate knowledge transfer when original owners transition into advisory roles.

   - Ensure a smooth handover, maintaining operational efficiency and strategic focus.

2. **Post-Acquisition Leadership Gaps:**

   - Address leadership gaps post-acquisition, aligning strategies, and facilitating seamless integrations.

# Depth of Engagement: How Far and Deep OPs Act as Interim Leaders

The responsibilities of OPs in interim CEO or CXO roles are comprehensive, covering both operational and strategic dimensions.

1. **Operational Leadership:**

   - Day-to-day operational oversight, ensuring continuity and efficiency.

   - Address immediate challenges and implement operational improvements.

2. **Strategic Decision-Making:**

   - Contribute to high-stakes strategic decision-making.

   - Drive organizational change, acting as change agents within portfolio companies.

Operating Partners emerge as instrumental leaders during periods of change and uncertainty within portfolio companies. Their engagements in interim CEO or CXO roles provide a strategic bridge, fostering stability, driving operational excellence, and guiding companies through transitions. By navigating these transitions with agility and depth, OPs contribute significantly to the resilience and growth of private equity-backed businesses.

# Ethical Dilemmas for Operating Partners

*"Whether in the Topline or Bottomline Hemisphere, A Strong Moral Compass Points North"*

*In the maze of moral challenges that businesses inevitably encounter, an Operating Partner (OP) must confront them head-on. The guiding principle is simple yet profound: "If you find yourself contemplating a decision, you're likely on the wrong path." A skilled OP is akin to a reliable compass, swiftly pointing north when faced with ethical dilemmas. Opting for the role of an Astrolabe, depending on external influences for direction, could lead to errors or, even worse, the perception of errors. It's a pragmatic reminder that in the murkier corners of business, decisive, ethically sound action is the beacon that illuminates the way forward.*

*So, be a compass, and rest easy; after all, Astrolabes are natural insomniacs!*

# The Ethics of Partnerships

Operating Partners (OPs) face unique ethical challenges in their roles, encompassing concerns related to conflicts of interest, employee treatment, and stakeholder communication. Here's a focused exploration of selected challenges (on inter alia basis):

| Ethical Challenge | Scenario | Dilemma |
|---|---|---|
| 1. Conflicts of Interest | The OP has a personal financial interest in a supplier or service provider. | Balancing personal relationships with fair decision-making in supplier selection. |
| 2. Employee Treatment and Layoffs | The OP is involved in decisions regarding employee layoffs during a restructuring. | Balancing financial imperatives with humane treatment and fair employment practices. |
| 3. Short-Term vs. Long-Term Value Creation | Pressure to deliver quick financial results to satisfy investors or meet targets. | Navigating the tension between short-term gains and sustainable, long-term value creation. |
| 5. Environmental and Social Impact | Operational decisions may have environmental or social implications. | Striking a balance between profitability and responsible business practices. |
| 8. Stakeholder Communication | Facing challenging decisions that impact various stakeholders. | Maintaining transparent and honest communication during periods of uncertainty. |

In addressing these challenges, OPs must prioritize ethical considerations. Transparency, fairness, and accountability should guide decision-making. Open communication with stakeholders, empathy in employee-related decisions, and a commitment to long-term sustainability can help OPs navigate these ethical dilemmas responsibly.

**77**

# The Darwin Prize for OPs

*Success readiness requires avoiding the slippery slopes of failure.*

*OPs are on a never-ending survival-of-the-fittest competition, where success awaits those who make the right decisions. However, OPs have their own set of anti-Key Success Factors (anti-KSF), just as evolution has its Darwin Awards, honouring those who follow the most unusual routes to failure. In this tongue-in-cheek manual for winning the "Darwin Prize for OPs," we expose the traps, the narrow paths, and the most reliable methods for gaining an honourable place in the hall of shame for OPs. Embrace this entertaining and educational list with a grain of salt; it will teach you how to smoothly fall from the peak of success to the valley of operational rejection.*

# The Anti-KSF

Below is the anti-KSF, a guide on the fastest and surest means to fail as an OP:

1. **Cultural Misalignment:**

   - Keep the Chip on your shoulder.

2. **Industry Ignorance:**

   - Stay too Lazy to Learn.

3. **Communication Breakdown:**

   - Keep the Poker Face.

4. **Resistance to Change:**

   - Not walking your own talk.

5. **Neglecting Morale:**

   - Remember, Empathy is not a weakness.

6. **Short-Term Focus:**

   - This is not your last role.

7. **Due Diligence Gaps:**

   - Take the role at face value.

8. **Stakeholder Neglect:**

   - This is not a multiple-choice quiz.

9. **Overpromising Results:**

   - The higher the jump, the harder the fall.

10. **Inability to Adapt:**

    - Dinosaurs are extinct by choice, not comet.

# ESG Integration

## Catalyst for Responsible Operational Value Creation (OVC)

"OPs who do not show signs of active ESG, are pronounced dead!"

*OPs who fail to display active embrace of ESG might as well be deemed extinct! Back in the 2000s, it was all about CSR, but fast forward to 2024, and the buzzword is ESG. As for the term in 2030, who knows. Perhaps my kids, the aficionados of cartoon songs, could christen it best and simplest: 'Clean, Fair, Share n Care. Sing with me!' The upgrade from CSR to ESG underscores a pivotal shift in corporate responsibility, emphasizing Environmental, Social, and Governance factors. It's not just about ticking boxes; it's about creating a harmonious melody of sustainability, fairness, and shared prosperity. In this dynamic landscape, embracing ESG isn't just a choice; it's embracing the tune of responsible business practices playing the soundtrack of the future. Free Advice: If you have a bad voice, just lip sync; everyone does it!"*

# ESG: The Beautiful Face of Deal Making

The landscape of Private Equity (PE) is undergoing a profound transformation with the ascendancy of Environmental, Social, and Governance (ESG) considerations. Within this dynamic paradigm, ESG principles are not mere checkboxes but integral elements shaping Operational Value Creation (OVC) strategies. The confluence of ESG and OVC represents a commitment by PE firms to responsible and sustainable business practices. Let's delve into a comprehensive exploration of how ESG considerations intricately influence OVC practices across the entire investment lifecycle:

## 1. *ESG as a Pre-Deal Imperative:*

- **Pre-Deal Due Diligence:** ESG is now a focal point in pre-deal assessments, scrutinizing potential portfolio companies for environmental impact, social responsibility, and governance structures. This involves navigating risks related to regulatory compliance, resource management, and social acceptability.

- **Strategic Investment Formulation:** ESG considerations play a pivotal role in shaping investment strategies. PE firms seek opportunities aligned with ESG goals, identifying businesses with sustainable practices to mitigate reputational risks and ensure enduring value creation.

## 2. *Operational Excellence Through an ESG Lens:*

- **Resource Efficiency:** OVC initiatives now actively enhance resource efficiency, minimizing waste, and optimizing energy consumption with a dual benefit of environmental alignment and operational cost reduction.

- **Social Impact Programs:** PE firms integrate social impact programs within OVC, fostering initiatives for workforce development, diversity and inclusion, and community engagement. These programs elevate the social responsibility profile of portfolio companies.

**81**

### 3. *ESG Metrics: Cornerstone of Performance Measurement:*

- **Incorporation of ESG Metrics:** ESG metrics are seamlessly woven into performance measurement frameworks for OVC. This allows PE firms to transparently track and assess the impact of operational improvements on ESG goals, providing stakeholders with a clear view of progress.

- **Linking ESG to Financial Performance:** There is a growing recognition that robust ESG performance can contribute to long-term financial success. PE firms explore ways to correlate ESG achievements with financial performance, creating a holistic approach to value creation.

### 4. *Governance as a Pillar of Ethical Practices:*

- **Board Diversity and Composition:** Governance improvements include efforts to augment board diversity, enhancing corporate governance, and positively impacting the reputation and sustainability of the business.

- **Ethical Supply Chain Practices:** OVC strategies scrutinize and enhance the ethical aspects of supply chain practices. Responsible sourcing, fair labor practices, and supply chain transparency contribute to enhanced governance.

### 5. *ESG as a Risk Mitigation Strategy:*

- **Reputational Risk Mitigation:** ESG integration within OVC serves as a proactive approach to mitigate reputational risks. Addressing environmental and social challenges helps build resilience against reputational damage, directly influencing the value of portfolio companies.

- **Regulatory Compliance:** Incorporating ESG factors into operational enhancements contributes to regulatory compliance, mitigating legal and regulatory risks that may arise due to non-compliance.

**6. *Investor and Stakeholder Expectations:***

- **Alignment with Investor Preferences:** Limited Partners (LPs) increasingly consider ESG factors in investment decisions. PE firms aligning OVC practices with ESG principles are better positioned to meet the expectations of socially responsible investors.

- **Stakeholder Engagement:** OVC strategies now incorporate stakeholder engagement plans, addressing the concerns and interests of a broader range of stakeholders, including employees, communities, and non-governmental organizations (NGOs).

**7. *Challenges and Opportunities:***

- **Data Standardization and Measurement:** Challenges include the lack of standardized ESG data and metrics. PE firms actively participate in initiatives to standardize reporting frameworks for better measurement.

- **Innovation and Competitive Advantage:** OVC practices embracing ESG considerations present opportunities for innovation and competitive advantage. Fostering a culture of responsible business practices can position portfolio companies more favorably in the marketplace.

The amalgamation of ESG principles with OVC strategies signifies a transformative shift towards sustainable and responsible investing in the PE industry. PE firms embracing these considerations are poised to create lasting positive impacts on portfolio companies, stakeholders, and the environment. Balancing financial returns with social and environmental responsibility is no longer just a regulatory requirement but a strategic imperative for long-term success in the evolving landscape of private equity.

In essence, the integration of ESG principles into OVC strategies reflects a broader commitment to responsible and sustainable business practices within the Private Equity industry. This shift aligns with the evolving expectations of investors, regulators, and society at large, positioning PE firms for sustainable success in an increasingly ESG-conscious world.

# Balancing Operational Value Creation Tools

*No "Cookie Cutters" for OVC!*

*Operational Value Creation (OVC) is no place for 'cookie cutters'! PE deals, much like the fancy funnel cakes, boast a delightful variety—never the same shape, consistency, or exact measures. It's this unpredictability that adds a dash of zing, akin to experimenting with different versions of one recipe. Operating Partners (OPs) find themselves in the role of busy chefs in busy diners, yearning to use cookie cutters but realizing they simply cannot—nor should they. The secret ingredient here is the oxymoron of 'structural flexibility.' This unique quality empowers OPs to skillfully navigate new challenges and situations. I once learned from my Civil Engineering Professor: Flexibility is Strength. A bamboo building that can sway will outlast rigid concrete structures. In the context of OVC, where the average OpCo faces seismic challenges akin to a Grade 7 earthquake twice a year, this structural flexibility emerges as the key to sustained resilience.*

## Striking the Balance Between Consistency and Flexibility

Despite the common claim of robust and standardized Operational Value Creation (OVC) frameworks in Private Equity (PE) firms, a closer inspection reveals significant variations among these approaches. This diversity suggests a critical area for improvement, prompting the assessment of the adequacy, depth, and consistency of these systems in driving a unified methodology and a structured approach.

| Approach | Key Characteristics |
| --- | --- |
| **Standardized OVC Framework** | - Ensures a consistent approach across diverse portfolio companies. |
| | - Implements streamlined processes for efficient and replicable execution. |
| | - Mitigates risks through the application of insights from past successes and lessons learned. |
| **OP Discretionary Autonomy** | - Tailors solutions to address unique challenges and capitalize on specific opportunities. |
| | - Demonstrates adaptability based on real-time assessments and changing circumstances. |
| | - Leverages the industry expertise of Operational Partners (OPs) for targeted and informed interventions. |
| **Hybrid Approach** | - Strikes a balance between the benefits of consistency and efficiency with the flexibility required for nuanced and industry-specific value creation. |
| | - Integrates elements from both standardized frameworks and OP discretionary autonomy, aligning with the distinct needs of each investment. |

The decision between these approaches is intricately linked to the PE firm's overall strategy, portfolio diversity, and the specific characteristics of each investment. While some firms prioritize a structured and consistent approach, others place high value on the flexibility and expertise offered by OPs' discretionary decision-making.

# Digital Transformation
## Unleashing Value with Operational Partners

In the fast-paced and technology-driven business landscape, digital transformation has become a critical driver of success and competitiveness. Private equity firms must recognize the importance of digital transformation in unlocking new opportunities, optimizing operations, and enhancing the value of portfolio companies. In this section, we will explore the role of operational partners in driving digital transformation initiatives within private equity and discuss potential caveats and special considerations related to this transformative journey.

The Power of Digital Transformation

Digital transformation refers to the strategic adoption and integration of digital technologies to revolutionize business processes and deliver enhanced value to stakeholders. It encompasses various elements, including automation, data analytics, artificial intelligence, cloud computing, and the Internet of Things (IoT). Embracing digital transformation empowers organizations to streamline operations, improve decision-making, enhance customer experiences, and create new business models and revenue streams.

# The Role of Operational Partners in Digital Transformation

Operational partners play a pivotal role in catalyzing and driving digital transformation initiatives within portfolio companies. Leveraging their industry expertise and operational acumen, operational partners work closely with management teams to navigate the complexities of digital transformation and maximize its potential value. Here are keyways in which operational partners contribute:

1. Digital Strategy Development: Operational partners collaborate with management teams to develop a clear digital strategy aligned with the goals and vision of the portfolio company. They assess the company's current digital capabilities, identify areas for improvement, and define a roadmap for digital transformation. Operational partners help prioritize investments, facilitate technology adoption, and ensure that the digital strategy aligns with the company's overall value creation objectives.

2. Operational Process Optimization: As digital transformation involves reimagining and optimizing operational processes, operational partners actively contribute their expertise in process improvement. They help identify opportunities for automation, digitization, and the integration of digital tools and technologies. Operational partners guide management teams in redesigning workflows, enhancing efficiency, and fostering a culture of continuous improvement.

3. Technology Assessment and Implementation: Operational partners assist in evaluating and selecting the appropriate digital technologies and tools that align with the portfolio company's unique needs. They conduct due diligence on vendors, assess the scalability and compatibility of solutions, and oversee the implementation process. Operational partners ensure smooth integration of digital technologies, minimize disruptions, and support change management efforts across the organization.

**88**

4. Data-Driven Decision Making: Digital transformation generates vast amounts of data that can be harnessed to drive informed decision-making. Operational partners work with management teams to define key performance indicators (KPIs) and establish robust data analytics capabilities. They help identify data sources, design dashboards and analytics frameworks, and facilitate the development of data-driven insights that empower strategic decision-making and value creation.

# Caveats and Special Considerations

While embarking on the digital transformation journey, private equity firms and their operational partners need to be mindful of certain caveats and special considerations. These include:

1. Talent Acquisition and Skill Enhancement: Digital transformation requires access to skilled talent capable of driving technological initiatives within the portfolio company. Operational partners collaborate with management teams to attract and develop digital expertise, either through recruitment or upskilling programs. They ensure that the company has the right talent in place to execute digital transformations successfully.

2. Change Management and Stakeholder Engagement: Digital transformation entails significant changes within an organization, affecting processes, roles, and responsibilities. Operational partners are responsible for managing and communicating these changes effectively. They provide guidance on change management strategies, facilitate stakeholder engagement, and align employee incentives and motivations with the goals of digital transformation.

3. Cybersecurity and Data Privacy: Digitally transformed businesses are often more vulnerable to cybersecurity threats and data breaches. Operational partners work closely with management teams to implement robust cybersecurity measures, assess risks, and ensure compliance with data protection regulations. They help establish processes and policies to mitigate cyber threats and safeguard sensitive data, ensuring the organization's resilience in the digital era.

Digital transformation has emerged as a crucial driver of success in today's business landscape. Private equity firms recognize the importance of this transformative journey and leverage the expertise of operational partners to drive digital initiatives within portfolio companies. By focusing on digital strategy, process optimization, technology implementation, and data-driven decision-making, operational partners unlock new value creation opportunities. While embarking on digital transformation, they must consider areas such as talent acquisition, change management, and cybersecurity to ensure a successful and secure transformation journey. With operational partners as catalysts, private equity firms can embrace digital transformation, optimize portfolio company operations, and create sustainable value in the digital era.

# Strategic Exit Planning

## An Operational Partner Perspective

*"Elvis has Left the Building just after The Eagle has Landed"!*

*Strategic Exit Planning is a performance fit for a king. Imagine this: Elvis has left the building just after the eagle has landed. It's not just a departure after a short visit; it's a skillful hype of the value of both acts: ease-in and ease-out; all is good when value is created. Operational Partners (OPs), with their subtle flair for theatrics, start spinning the 'Go to Market' narrative the moment they take "ownership" of the OpCo. Just like Elvis, they see a 100 of different ways to exit the building, and all are good, for value has been created.*

# The Importance of Strategic Exit Planning

Strategic exit planning is a critical component of value creation in private equity. It involves developing a well-thought-out strategy to maximize returns on investments and optimize the exit process. Effective exit planning requires careful consideration of various factors, including market conditions, industry dynamics, and the unique characteristics of portfolio companies. In this section, we explore the different exit routes and strategies, as well as the vital role that operational partners play in achieving successful exits.

Strategic exit planning is not a mere afterthought; it is an integral part of the investment journey. As a matter of fact, it is the only true and common objective of all investment journeys. By carefully planning the exit from the outset, private equity firms can increase the likelihood of generating substantial returns for investors. Moreover, a well-executed exit can have a significant impact on a firm's reputation and future deal sourcing opportunities. It allows for the efficient deployment of capital and the ability to redeploy funds into new investments.

# Exit Routes: A Spectrum of Options

In the realm of private equity, there exists a diverse array of exit routes that investors can consider. The choice of the most suitable exit route depends on various factors, including industry dynamics, company performance, market conditions, and investor objectives. Let's explore some common exit routes:

1.  Initial Public Offering (IPO): An IPO involves taking a private company public by listing it on a stock exchange. This route offers liquidity and access to public markets, allowing investors to capture the full potential of the company's value. Operational partners, in partnership with management teams, play a crucial role in preparing the portfolio company for the rigors of going public, including financial reporting compliance, governance enhancements, and investor relations strategies.

2.  Secondary Sale: A secondary sale involves selling the ownership stake in the portfolio company to another investor or a strategic buyer. This exit route offers flexibility and allows for the realization of the investment without the costs and scrutiny associated with an IPO. Operational partners contribute by positioning the company for optimal valuation, conducting due diligence on potential buyers, and navigating complex negotiations.

3.  Management Buyout (MBO) or Management Buy-In (MBI): In an MBO, the existing management team acquires the majority or entire ownership of the company, often with the support of private equity financing. An MBI, on the other hand, involves an external management team acquiring the business. Operational partners can play a critical role in assisting management teams with financial modeling, structuring the deal, and providing guidance during the transition period.

4.  Recapitalization: Recapitalization involves altering the capital structure of the portfolio company, typically by introducing debt financing or refinancing existing debt. This strategy allows for the

extraction of value while retaining partial ownership. Operational partners contribute by optimizing the company's financial position, identifying potential debt financing options, and negotiating favorable terms.

5. Strategic Sale: A strategic sale involves selling the portfolio company to a strategic acquirer within the same industry or a complementary sector. This exit route provides an opportunity to leverage synergies, access new markets, and unlock additional value. Operational partners play a critical role in positioning the company as an attractive acquisition target, conducting thorough due diligence, and ensuring a smooth transition post-acquisition.

# The Role of Operational Partners in Strategic Exit Planning

Operational Partners, with their deep industry knowledge, operational expertise, and hands-on approach, are invaluable when it comes to strategic exit planning. They play a crucial role in maximizing value creation throughout the investment lifecycle, including during the exit planning phase. Their involvement may include:

1. Financial Performance Optimization: Operational partners work closely with management teams to identify and implement strategic initiatives that drive revenue growth, improve profitability, and enhance operational efficiency. By helping the portfolio company achieve robust financial performance, operational partners contribute to a higher valuation at the time of exit.

2. Governance and Compliance: Operational partners assist in strengthening corporate governance practices and ensuring compliance with relevant regulations. This includes implementing robust internal controls, enhancing transparency, and addressing any potential risk areas that may impact the valuation or attractiveness of the company to potential buyers.

3. Scalability and Growth Potential: Operational partners collaborate with management teams to identify opportunities for expansion and accelerate growth. They help optimize the company's operations, refine its business model, and explore new markets or product lines. By demonstrating the company's scalability and growth potential, operational partners enhance its attractiveness during the exit process.

4. Relationship with Potential Buyers: Operational partners leverage their industry networks and relationships to identify potential buyers and facilitate introductions. They provide valuable insights and market intelligence, helping potential acquirers understand the strategic value and growth prospects of the portfolio company.

# Special Considerations in Exit Planning

## Admin, Tactical, and Strategic

During the exit planning process in private equity, there are several special considerations or caveats where operational partners can play a crucial role. Let's explore some of these aspects:

1. Data Room Management: Operational partners take the lead in managing the comprehensive data room that potential buyers require to evaluate the portfolio company. They ensure that all necessary documentation is organized, accurate, and readily accessible. Operational partners provide insights into the key value drivers and help potential buyers fully understand the company's performance, growth potential, and risks involved.

2. Developing Accurate Projections: Operational partners collaborate with management teams to develop realistic and comprehensive projections for the portfolio company's financial performance over the next 3-5 years. These projections play a vital role in the valuation and pricing of the acquisition. By aligning projections with buyer expectations and demonstrating a compelling growth story, operational partners enhance the chances of a successful and value-maximizing exit.

3. Deal Structure and Incentives: Operational partners guide negotiations on deal structures, including considerations like golden handshakes or golden parachutes for key executives or management teams. They strike a balance between incentivizing management for a smooth transition and safeguarding the overall value creation objectives and financial prudence.

4. Synergy Assessment and Integration Planning: Operational partners collaborate with management teams to assess and

**97**

articulate the potential synergies that can enhance the value of the portfolio company. They develop integration plans that outline how the portfolio company will seamlessly merge with the buyer's operations, capturing the anticipated synergies and minimizing any potential disruptions.

5. Smooth Transition and Stakeholder Communication: Operational partners play a pivotal role in facilitating a smooth transition from private equity ownership to the buyer, ensuring continuity of operations, and minimizing any disruptions that may impact the company's performance or value. They manage stakeholder communication during the transition, ensure transparency, build trust, and address any concerns that may arise among employees, customers, or suppliers.

Hence, strategic exit planning is a key component of value creation in private equity. By considering the various exit routes, understanding the unique characteristics of portfolio companies, and leveraging the expertise of operational partners, private equity firms can successfully navigate through the exit process and maximize returns for investors. Successful exits not only generate substantial value but also enhance a firm's reputation and pave the way for future investment opportunities. With careful planning, execution, and collaboration with operational partners, private equity firms can unlock the full potential of their investments and leave a lasting impact in the dynamic world of deal-making.

# The Racing Car Dilemma: Driver vs. Mechanic

The need for Operational Partners (OPs) in Private Equity is best illustrated by the Racing Car Dilemma: Mechanic vs. Driver. In high-speed races, both the driver and mechanic must understand each other's roles, acting as mirrors to one another. However, within the rapid and dynamic time frame of a race, a driver cannot effectively assume the role of a mechanic, and vice versa. This parallels the situation many Operating Companies (OpCos) face when hiring a CEO. There's a common misconception that CEOs should be both "Fix-it" and "Drive-it" experts, which is rarely the reality. Traditional CEOs often excel at either driving well-established systems or fixing and improving businesses in need, but not both. Enter the OP – a "Driver-Mechanic" hybrid capable of simultaneously driving and fixing. It's not just playing with words; OPs genuinely possess the unique ability to seamlessly transition from under the hood to behind the wheel. They are akin to asking a McKinsey consultant to run an automotive production plant or tasking an ER doctor to devise a plan for emergency healthcare improvements. Remarkably, OPs deliver on both fronts, showcasing their capacity to transcend roles with exceptional skill.

# PART 3 :

# The Merit-driven Value Management System Solution

# Merit-driven Value Management System (mVMS)

## The Need for a Standardized VMS (Value Management System)

Navigating the complex landscape of private equity (PE) and investment management demands a novel approach to value creation, one that transcends ad-hoc methodologies and embraces systematic innovation. Enter the Merit-driven Value Management System (VMS), a groundbreaking framework designed to serve not only as a management tool for strategic planning but also as a dynamic platform for continuous learning and knowledge transfer.

_NOTE: While I am using the Merit-driven notion or description of the VMS and other frameworks, this is meant to be adapted by the user for any adjective they see fit. To my mind, all OVC activities need be merit-driven._

## A Unified Approach to Value Management

In an industry where bespoke strategies often prevail, the Merit-driven VMS introduces a standardized and structured system, addressing the need for a unified approach to value management. Many PE firms and investors, while possessing individualized methods, may lack a cohesive framework to guide their endeavors systematically. The VMS fills this void by offering a holistic system that streamlines processes, ensures consistency, and injects innovation into the fabric of value creation.

**101**

# Dynamic Ecosystem for Comprehensive Value Enhancement

At its essence, the VMS is not just a set of principles; it is a dynamic ecosystem that adapts to the ever-evolving needs of businesses, industries, and growth stages. It brings together strategic planning, operational efficiency, talent management, risk mitigation, and innovation, providing a comprehensive guide to enhance the performance and value proposition of portfolio companies.

## Innovative Elements in Value Creation

What sets the Merit-driven VMS apart is its integration of innovative elements into each stage of the value creation process. From operational value creation (OVC) to TVC metrics, the Merit-driven Operating Model (mOM), and the Portfolio Optimization and Periodization Process (POPP), the VMS addresses intricate components that significantly contribute to informed decision-making, strategic planning, and resource allocation.

# A Learning and Knowledge Transfer Platform

Crucially, the Merit-driven VMS functions not only as a management tool but also as a powerful learning and knowledge transfer platform. Recognizing the importance of continuous improvement and knowledge dissemination, the VMS facilitates the transfer of best practices, lessons learned, and strategic insights across the entire investment lifecycle.

# Structured Journey and Continuous Learning

Value creation, according to the mVMS, is a nuanced and dynamic process that requires both adaptability and structure. The framework's strength lies in its ability to guide stakeholders through a structured journey—from initial business evaluation through strategic planning and execution to sustainable growth. Simultaneously, it acts as a conduit for the transfer of institutional knowledge, fostering a culture of continuous learning within organizations.

# A Paradigm Shift in Value Creation

In conclusion, Merit-driven VMS heralds a paradigm shift in the approach to value creation within private equity and investment management. Beyond being a management tool, it serves as a beacon for structured innovation and a platform for continuous learning. As the financial landscape continues to evolve, the VMS stands as a catalyst for elevating the standards of value management, shaping a future where structured approaches and continuous learning intertwine in the pursuit of enduring value.

# Applicability Across Industries and Leadership Roles

Moreover, the applicability of the Merit-driven Value Management System (mVMS) extends beyond the realm of private equity, reaching into the domains of CEOs, startup founders, and entrepreneurs. While initially tailored for the high standards of active investment management within PE firms, the mVMS encapsulates a mindset and approach that transcends industry boundaries. It emphasizes the significance of discipline, rigor, and a resolute will to succeed, characteristics that are universally relevant in the business landscape. Whether navigating the complexities of a multi-billion-dollar portfolio or steering a fledgling startup toward growth, the mVMS instills a culture of excellence, accountability, and strategic clarity. It underscores the notion that success is not just about individual achievement but, more importantly, about creating an environment where others can thrive and succeed collaboratively. In essence, the VMS serves as a beacon for those who seek not just success but a sustainable and impactful legacy in the dynamic world of business.

Navigating the complex landscape of private equity (PE) and investment management demands a streamlined and novel approach to value creation, one that transcends ad-hoc methodologies and embraces systematic innovation. Enter the Merit-driven Value Management System (mVMS), a trailblazing framework designed to serve not only as a management tool for strategic planning but also as a dynamic platform for continuous learning and knowledge transfer.

In an industry where bespoke strategies often prevail, the Merit-driven VMS introduces a standardized and structured system and a unified approach, addressing the need for a unified approach to value management. Many PE firms and investors, while possessing individualized methods, may lack a cohesive framework to guide their endeavors systematically. The mVMS fills this void by offering a holistic system that streamlines processes, ensures consistency, and injects innovation into the fabric of value creation. Akin of throwing a rock in still and murky waters, this proposal is a call for change.

At its essence, the mVMS is not just a set of principles; it is a dynamic ecosystem that adapts to the ever-evolving needs of businesses, industries, and growth stages. It brings together strategic planning, operational efficiency, talent management, risk mitigation, and innovation, providing a comprehensive guide to enhance the performance and value proposition of portfolio companies.

What sets the Merit-driven mVMS apart is its integration of innovative elements into each stage of the value creation process. From operational value creation (OVC) to total value creation (TVC) metrics, the Merit-driven Operating Model (mOM), and the Portfolio Optimization and Periodization Process (POPP), the VMS addresses intricate components that significantly contribute to informed decision-making, strategic planning, and resource allocation.

Crucially, the Merit-driven VMS functions not only as a management tool but also as a powerful learning and knowledge transfer platform. Recognizing the importance of continuous improvement and knowledge dissemination, the mVMS facilitates the transfer of best practices, lessons learned, and strategic insights across the entire investment life cycle. It serves as a repository of valuable experiences, ensuring that the expertise gained from one venture informs and enhances the strategies employed in subsequent ones.

Value creation, according to the mVMS, is a nuanced and dynamic process that requires both adaptability and structure. The framework's strength lies in its ability to guide stakeholders through a structured journey—from initial business evaluation through strategic planning and execution to sustainable growth. Simultaneously, it acts as a conduit for the transfer of institutional knowledge, fostering a culture of continuous learning within organizations.

In conclusion, Merit-driven VMS heralds a paradigm shift in the approach to value creation within private equity and investment management. Beyond being a management tool, it serves as a beacon for structured innovation and a platform for continuous learning. As the financial landscape continues to evolve, the mVMS stands as a catalyst for elevating the standards of value management, shaping a future where structured approaches and continuous learning intertwine in the pursuit of enduring value.

Moreover, the applicability of the Merit-driven Value Management System (mVMS) extends beyond the realm of private equity, reaching into the domains of CEOs, startup founders, and entrepreneurs. While initially tailored for the high standards of active investment management within PE firms, the mVMS encapsulates a mindset and approach that transcends industry boundaries. It emphasizes the significance of discipline, rigor, and a resolute will to succeed, characteristics that are universally relevant in the business landscape. Whether navigating the complexities of a multi-billion-dollar portfolio or steering a fledgling startup toward growth, the mVMS instills a culture of excellence, accountability, and strategic clarity. It underscores the notion that success is not just about individual achievement but, more importantly, about creating an environment where others can thrive and succeed collaboratively. In essence, the mVMS serves as a beacon for those who seek not just success but a sustainable and impactful legacy in the dynamic world of business.

A proprietary and original approach to Value Creation.

# The Merit-driven Value Management System®

 **The 7 Pillars of our mVMS ®**

### 1. Business Baseline
Current Issues. Business Performance.
Baseline Metrics. In-Depth Analytics.

### 2. Opportunities Outline
Quick Wins. Improvement Projects.
Resources and Timelines.

### 5. Value Delivery
Steadfast Delivery. Performance
Benchmarks. Measurable and
Traceable. Impactful and Meaningful.

### 3. Value Flywheel
Sustainable Levers. Prioritization
and Gating. Sustained Growth.

### 6. Business Remodeling
Necessary Pivots. Strategic Transformations.
Value-driven Growth. Resilience Autopilot.

### 4. Executive Excellence
Fortified Leadership. Business
Coaching. Interim and Fractional.
Talent Acquisition.

### 7. Knowledge Transfer
Active Collaboration. C-Suite Empowerment.
Continuous Improvement. Strategic Agility.

# The mVMS Solution

I have developed the concept for Merit-driven Value Management System or mVMS a comprehensive system aimed at driving value across various facets of business, covering aspects from baseline evaluation, and implementation excellence to knowledge transfer.

It is comprised of two distinct layers:

# Layer 1- The Drivers:

# Approach and Methodologies

### 1) The Approach - Total Value Creation (TVC)

The TVC approach serves as the foundational philosophy within mVMS. It encompasses the comprehensive strategy for Operating Partners and CEOs working in Private Equity (PE) Portfolio Companies. The focus is on maximizing shareholder value and achieving sustainable financial success through a systematic and integrated set of strategies.

### 2) The Methodology – The Merit-driven Operating Model (mOM)

The Merit-driven Operating Model (mOM) is an evolving methodology designed to complement the TVC approach. It provides a structured and systematic framework for implementing the TVC strategies. mOM will define the specific processes, procedures, and guidelines that Operating Partners and CEOs can follow to execute the Total Value Creation approach effectively.


While I am using the Approach and Methodology to refer to TVC and mOM; one can simple adapt TVC as the rationale or philosophy behind the mVMS and mOM as the process outline.

# Layer 2 - The Enablers:

# Frameworks and Toolkits

Layer 2 of the mVMS comprises various frameworks and toolkits that offer practical guidance and resources for implementing the TVC approach within the mOM methodology. These frameworks and toolkits provide actionable insights and structured approaches to address specific aspects of value management. Here are few key components (on inter-alia basis):

1. **The Merit-driven Operating Partner Playbook (mOPP)**

   - A comprehensive guide outlining best practices, strategies, and tools for Operating Partners to excel in their roles within the private equity landscape.

2. **Portfolio Optimization and Periodization Process (POPP)**

   - A strategic process that helps optimize the composition of the portfolio, considering market conditions, risk factors, and value creation opportunities over defined periods.

3. **Scale and Scope Optimization Framework (SSOF)**

   - A framework designed to assess and optimize the scale and scope of portfolio companies, ensuring they are aligned with market demands and strategic objectives.

4. **Balanced ValueCard (BVC)**

   - A strategic management tool that aligns with Total Value Creation (TVC) principles, providing a holistic framework and dashboard for Operating Partners (OPs) to set targets and assess performance on a comprehensive basis.

5. **Value Engine Flywheel (VEF):**

- A dynamic toolkit that facilitates the continuous generation of value by identifying key drivers and fostering a cyclical process of innovation, efficiency, and growth.

Each element within Layer 2 provides practical tools and frameworks that align with the TVC approach and are guided by the mOM methodology. This dual-layered structure ensures a holistic and practical approach to value management within the private equity value creation ecosystem.

# mVMS in Q&A Form

In straightforward terms, the mVMS serves as a comprehensive and validated mechanism supporting Operating Partners (OPs) across strategy, design, and implementation levels. Here's a breakdown of how each tool or system within the mVMS addresses specific needs:

| What Does an OP Need? | The Solutions |
|---|---|
| Need a robust system to manage the complete Value Creation process and coordinate with the PE sponsor and other stakeholders? | mVMS<br><br>Value Management System |
| Need to streamline a consistent and continuous approach to Value Creation? | TVC<br>Total Value Creation |
| >>> The Why and How | |
| Need to define a clear scope and resource allocation with clear targets for Value Creation? | mOM<br><br>Operating Model |
| >>> The What, Who, When ... | |
| Need a diverse set of tools and frameworks to facilitate the Value Creation process? | mOPP<br><br>Operating Partner Playbook |
| >>> Not to reinvent the Wheel! | |
| Need to take a step back and decide which portfolio to focus on and assess the potency of the value creation process? | POPP<br><br>Portfolio Optimization and Periodization Process |
| >>> Stop and Ask Why? | |
| Need to optimize the Value Creation process and balance resource allocation in terms of Scope and Scale? | SSOF |

**112**

| >>> Why this and not that! | Scale and Scope Optimization Framework |
|---|---|
| Need to have a clear Dashboard and Radar to have a holistic overview of results?<br><br>>>> How are we Doin'! | BVC<br><br>Balanced ValueCard |
| Need ideas and a primer on potential Value Creation levers?<br><br>>>> The What, What, and more What! | VEF<br><br>Value Engine Framework |

In essence, the mVMS offers a tailored solution to various OP needs, providing a structured and practical approach to drive value creation across the private equity landscape.

A comprehensive set of proprietary frameworks and tools.

# The mVMS Toolbox

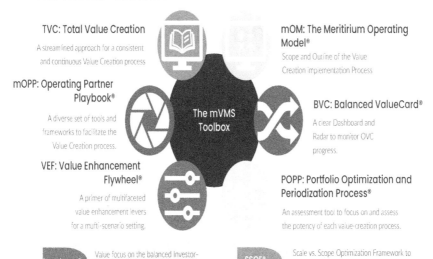

**TVC: Total Value Creation**

A streamlined approach for a consistent and continuous Value Creation process

**mOPP: Operating Partner Playbook®**

A diverse set of tools and frameworks to facilitate the Value Creation process.

**VEF: Value Enhancement Flywheel®**

A primer of multifaceted value enhancement levers for a multi-scenario setting.

**mOM: The Meritirium Operating Model®**

Scope and Outline of the Value Creation implementation Process

**BVC: Balanced ValueCard®**

A clear Dashboard and Radar to monitor OVC progress.

**POPP: Portfolio Optimization and Periodization Process®**

An assessment tool to focus on and assess the potency of each value-creation process.

**Investomer®** — Value focus on the balanced Investor-Customer-centric business model.

**SSOF®** — Scale vs. Scope Optimization Framework to balance resource allocation.

**114**

# Layer 1 - The Drivers

# Approach and Methodologies

# Total Value Creation Framework: Detailed Overview

## A Conceptual Innovative Framework for Operating Partner Accelerated and Sustained Growth

Total Value Creation (TVC) for Operating Partners and CEOs working at Private Equity (PE) Portfolio Companies involves a tailored approach that aligns with the specific goals and dynamics of the private equity environment. The key focus is on maximizing shareholder value and achieving sustainable financial success.

The Key Success Factors for any TVC Approach:

- Continuous Process
- Collaborative Framework
- Data-Driven Edge
- Principal Mindset  (vs. Agent)
- Unified Leadership
- Investomer Focus (Investor / Customer)

116

# The 13 elements for Total Value Creation

1. **Investor Value Focus:**

   - Prioritize activities that directly contribute to increasing shareholder value. Align strategies, operational improvements, and decision-making to maximize returns for investors.

2. **Strategic Alignment with PE Objectives:**

   - Ensure that the overall corporate strategy is closely aligned with the objectives and exit strategies of the private equity firm. This involves understanding the investment thesis and working collaboratively to achieve shared goals.

3. **Operational Excellence:**

   - Implement operational efficiency measures that directly impact the bottom line. Streamline processes, reduce costs, and optimize resource utilization to enhance overall profitability.

4. **Financial Performance Metrics:**

   - Emphasize financial KPIs such as EBITDA growth, cash flow generation, and return on investment. Regularly monitor and report on these metrics to demonstrate the financial health and success of the portfolio company.

5. **Exit Readiness:**

   - Develop and maintain a focus on being exit-ready at all times. This includes improving the market position, financial stability, and overall attractiveness of the portfolio company to potential buyers.

6. **Market and Industry Dynamics:**

- Stay informed about market trends, industry disruptions, and competitive landscapes. Anticipate and adapt to changes to position the company for sustained success and value creation.

7. **Risk Management and Mitigation:**
   - Implement robust risk management strategies to identify and mitigate potential threats to the business. This involves initiative-taking planning to address challenges that may impact the value of the portfolio company.

8. **Intrinsic Scalability:**
   - Develop a business model that can expand into new markets, product lines, or customer segments without a complete overhaul. A scalable business model allows for strategic diversification and ensures that the company can explore growth opportunities without compromising efficiency.

9. **Relationships with Stakeholders:**
   - Foster strong relationships not only with investors but also with other stakeholders such as customers, suppliers, and employees. Positive relationships contribute to overall business stability and growth.

10. **Innovative Solutions and Differentiation:**
    - Encourage a culture of innovation within the organization. Seek opportunities for product or service differentiation that can enhance the company's market position and value proposition.

11. **Talent Management and Leadership Development:**
    - Invest in developing leadership capabilities within the organization. Ensure a strong and capable management team that can drive the company's strategic objectives and navigate complex challenges.

**118**

12. **Adaptability to PE Lifecycle:**

- Recognize the unique lifecycle stages of a private equity investment (acquisition, value creation, and exit). Tailor strategies and actions to each stage, considering the evolving needs and expectations of the PE firm.

13. **Communication and Transparency:**

- Maintain open and transparent communication with the private equity firm. Regularly update them on the progress, challenges, and achievements of the portfolio company, fostering a collaborative and trusting relationship.

By integrating these elements, Total Value Creation for Operating Partners and CEOs in the private equity context becomes a comprehensive strategy to drive financial success and enhance the overall value of the portfolio company.

As opposed to the common understanding what TVC is, as in stakeholder-wide vs. investor-wide, my suggested meaning is more toward a Continuous and Wholistic, i.e. covering beyond the OVC (pos-acquisition) cycle and on full engagement, full plan-achieve-measure-repeat loop.

# The PUSH Excellence Make Value Right Model (PEMVR)

In order to simplify the TVC approach, this book recommends a Multi-Stage Framework that provides a systematic and active approach to drive exponential growth and value creation for portfolio companies.

By adopting the PEMVR Multi-Stage Framework, Operating Partners actively engage with portfolio companies, driving targeted actions aligned with the broader goal of creating sustained value.

## Escalating Effort & Timeline

| Level / Lever | P ush (for) | E xcellence | M ake | V alue | R ight |
|---------------|-------------|-------------|-------|--------|--------|
| **Stage 1** | Product | EBITDA (Acceleration) | Mix | Volume | Risks |
| **Stage 2** | Pricing | Efficiencies | Market | Value-Add | Remedy |
| **Stage 3** | Pivot | Economics (Scale & Scope) | Model (Business) | Venture (Blitz of Innovation) | Restructure |
| **Stage 4** | Platform | Exit | Maximize (Returns) OVC to TVC | Valuation (Model) | Rewards (& Reporting) |

# Stage 1: Product, Volume and Mix Optimization

1. **PUSH for EBITDA Acceleration:**

   - *Objective:* Actively identify and implement strategies to enhance the company's EBITDA performance.

   - *Key Focus Areas:* Operational efficiencies, cost controls, and revenue maximization.

2. **Excellence in Mix and Volume:**

   - *Objective:* Analyze and optimize the product mix and sales volume to maximize revenue and profitability.

   - *Key Focus Areas:* Market segmentation, product portfolio analysis, and sales strategy.

3. **Maximize Value Right by Mitigating Risks:**

   - *Objective:* Proactively address potential risks and uncertainties that could impact the company's value.

   - *Key Focus Areas:* Risk assessment, mitigation strategies, and resilience planning.

# Stage 2: Balancing Scale and Scope in Market Expansion

4. **Drive Pricing Efficiencies:**

    - *Objective:* Optimize pricing strategies to maximize revenue and maintain competitiveness in the market.

    - *Key Focus Areas:* Pricing analysis, competitive positioning, and value-based pricing.

5. **Create Market Value-Add:**

    - *Objective:* Identify opportunities to add value to the market, enhancing the company's competitive positioning.

    - *Key Focus Areas:* Market analysis, customer needs identification, and value proposition enhancement.

6. **Remedial Actions for Enhanced Performance:**

    - *Objective:* Implement corrective measures to address any challenges faced during this stage.

    - *Key Focus Areas:* Continuous improvement, performance monitoring, and adaptive strategies.

# Stage 3: Business Model Pivot and Innovation

7. **Scaling and Expanding Economics:**

    - *Objective:* Identify opportunities to scale the business model and explore new scopes for growth.

    - *Key Focus Areas:* Scalability assessment, market expansion, and growth potential analysis.

8. **Business Model Transformation:**

    - *Objective:* Encourage a venture-driven approach to innovation, fostering new disruptive ideas.

    - *Key Focus Areas:* Innovation culture, R&D initiatives, and business model innovation.

9. **Restructure for Enhanced Efficiency:**

    - *Objective:* Evaluate and implement organizational changes to streamline operations and adapt to market demands.

    - *Key Focus Areas:* Organizational structure, process optimization, and talent alignment.

# Stage 4: Platform Readiness and Maximized Returns

10. **Exit Strategy Execution:**

- *Objective:* Plan and execute a strategic exit to unlock the maximum value for all stakeholders.

- *Key Focus Areas:* Exit planning, stakeholder communication, and value realization.

11. **Maximize Returns with Optimal Valuation and Capitalization:**

- *Objective:* Ensure the company is appropriately valued and capitalized to optimize returns.

- *Key Focus Areas:* Financial optimization, valuation analysis, and capital structure refinement.

12. **Reporting and Rewarding Success:**

- *Objective:* Establish transparent reporting mechanisms to celebrate achievements and reward key contributors.

- *Key Focus Areas:* Performance metrics, reporting frameworks, and incentive structures.

*Stages are not chronologically ordered but rather an escalation process of effort and resources. Some businesses and industries can choose a different staging order or full matrix re-ordering.*

# The Generic PEMVR Cycle®

The PUSH Excellence Make Value Right Model (PEMVR) provides a systematic and active approach to drive exponential growth and value creation for portfolio companies and can be led by either external or in-house support.

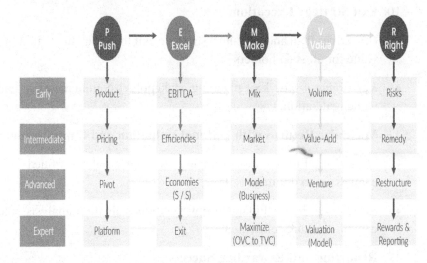

| | P<br>Push | E<br>Excel | M<br>Make | V<br>Value | R<br>Right |
|---|---|---|---|---|---|
| Early | Product | EBITDA | Mix | Volume | Risks |
| Intermediate | Pricing | Efficiencies | Market | Value-Add | Remedy |
| Advanced | Pivot | Economies (S / S) | Model (Business) | Venture | Restructure |
| Expert | Platform | Exit | Maximize (OVC to TVC) | Valuation (Model) | Rewards & Reporting |

# TVC Metrics: OVC Potency

## Total Value Creation (TVC) Calculation

TVC=Cash Created=Entry Discount+Exit Expansion+OVC+Synergy (in $ terms)

VC Waterfall / Bridge Stacking to 100%:

TVC Waterfall=X%(Entry Discount)+Y%(Exit Expansion)+Z%(OVC)+S%(Synergy - only for funds or networks)TVC Waterfall=$X$%(Entry Discount)+$Y$%(Exit Expansion)+$Z$%(OVC)+$S$%(Synergy - for funds or networks)

Where:

- $X$% --- Market Discount, Financial Structure, Leverage

- $Y$% --- Market Premium, Exit Route, Packaging

- $S$% --- Synergy Effect; Fund Positive Network

- $Z$% --- The effective OVC

# OVC Potency Measure

OVC Potency Measure=m $Z / (X+Y+Z+S)$%

Typically, OVC Potency needs to be greater than 80%. Operating Partners can influence contributions from Y, S, and Z, while the Deal Team can influence contributions from X, Y, and S.

**Notes:**

1.  The typical acquisition valuation metrics may be skewed by a "Hockey Stick" fallacy, necessitating corrective OVC as a key remedy.

2.  In any disciplined scenario, valuations should be based on a Parity Basis, where there are no assumed or embedded multiple expansions or contractions (arbitrage).

# TVC and the TVC Waterfall / Bridge

TVC $=$ Cash Created $=$ Entry Discount $+$ Exit Expansion$+$ OVC $+$ Synergy (in $ terms)

TVC Waterfall / Bridge stack to 100%

TVC Waterfall $=$ X% (Entry Discount) $+$ Y% (Exit Expansion)$+$ Z% (OVC) $+$ S%(Synergy - only for funds or networks)

Using the above approach, we can envisage a measure for OVC potency.

OVC Potency Measure $=$ Z/(X+Y+Z+S)%

Typically, OVC Potency needs to be $> 80\%$

Operating Partner can influence Y, S, and Z contributions.

Deal Team can influence X, Y and S contributions.

**Notes:**

1) The typical acquisition valuation metrics are skewed by a "Hockey Stick" fallacy/illusion, whereby corrective OVC is needed as a key remedy
2) In any disciplined scenario, valuations should be based on a Parity Basis whereby there are no assumed or embedded multiple expansion or contraction (arbitrage)

**128**

# The Emergence of the Investomer

### Balancing Investor and Customer Interests

In today's dynamic business landscape, the traditional demarcation between investors and customers is undergoing a transformative shift, giving rise to what can be aptly termed the "Investomer." This conceptual fusion represents a congruence of Investor and Customer, encapsulating a paradigm where business decisions are intricately woven around delivering benefits not only to shareholders but also to the end consumers. The Investomer philosophy challenges the notion that one's gains must come at the expense of the other's losses. Instead, it asserts that a sustainable business platform must navigate the delicate balance between investor returns and customer value.

A cornerstone of the Investomer philosophy is the acknowledgment that prioritizing one group over the other is a short-sighted approach. Sustainable growth necessitates a strategic equilibrium where the interests of investors and customers are not seen as conflicting but rather as symbiotic. For instance, while lowering prices may offer immediate benefits to customers, a wise and sustainable business understands that this strategy can lead to a domino effect—concentrated suppliers, business shutdowns, or compromised product quality in the long run. The Investomer mindset rejects the notion that success can be achieved by sacrificing one side for the benefit of the other, recognizing that a harmonious growth and gain is pivotal for sustained prosperity.

Investomer-driven decision-making is rooted in the understanding that long-term success requires a holistic perspective, considering the intertwined interests of both investors and customers. By aligning business strategies with the Investomer ethos, leaders and operating partners can foster an environment where the pursuit of financial returns goes hand in hand with delivering value to end consumers. This approach not only ensures the longevity of the business but also contributes to the broader goal of creating an ecosystem where both investors and customers thrive synergistically.

# The Rise of the Investomer®

Maximum valuations can only be attained via balanced focus on both the customer and investor; any misguided shortsight to the needs of any will have a profound impact.

**Customer Focus**

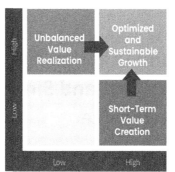

| | |
|---|---|
| Unsustainable | Ideal Growth Platform |
| Lower ROI | Balanced ST and LT Goals |
| OpCo CF Stress | Maximum Value Realization |
| Ex: RIM | (DCF vs Multiples) |
| | Ex: Amazon, Costco, Tesla |

| | |
|---|---|
| Business Risks | Hockey Stick Fallacy |
| Struggling P&L, CF | Difficult to Sell |
| and BS | Struggling S&M function |
| Death Spiral Launch | Financial Engineering |
| Pad | Competitive Risks |
| | Reputational Risks |
| | Ex: VW Tests, Apple Battery |

**Investor Focus**

# The Merit-driven Operating Model – mOM

"Think mOMentum!"

## A Systematic and Creative Approach to Achieving Consistent and Simplified Operational Excellence

The Merit-driven Operating Model is the foundational framework that drives a relentless commitment to operational excellence and consistency. Engineered to foster efficiency, spur innovation, and cultivate sustainable growth, MOM is a dynamic architectural foundation that adapts to evolving business needs, industries, and growth stages, empowering organizations to thrive amid dynamic market conditions.

To lead a consistent Total Value Management process, the Operating Model comprises seven integrated circular stages:

**1. Business Baseline: Unveiling the Canvas** Begin with a brushstroke of comprehensive evaluation, unveiling the canvas of baseline metrics. Analyze the present state of your business, exploring its performance, capabilities, and untapped potential. This initial stroke sets the stage, revealing the colors of strengths, weaknesses, and unexplored landscapes.

**2. Opportunities Outline: Painting Future Perspectives** This stage is an artist's palette, profiling improvement opportunities with strokes that distinguish between Quick Wins, Rapid Improvements, and Breakthroughs. The canvas is outlined, and resources are blended in hues, strategically aligned with your business's objectives. Each stroke crafts a pathway for enhancement that seamlessly integrates with your strategic vision.

**3. Value Flywheel: Brushing mOMentum Into Strategy** Craft a methodical plan that brushes mOMentum into your business objectives. The Value Flywheel isn't just a stroke; it's a series of deliberate strokes that create a masterpiece of immediate success and sustained growth. Each stroke adds depth, ensuring your initiatives contribute to a canvas of perpetual motion and strategic brilliance.

**4. Executive Excellence: Sculpting Leadership Fortitude** This stage is akin to sculpting leadership fortitude, shaping leaders capable of steering your business toward value-driven success. It's not just about filling positions; it's about carving out leaders who become the sculptures of your organizational narrative. Every chisel is deliberate, cultivating leadership as a masterpiece in its own right.

**5. Value Delivery: Infusing Tangible Realities** Ensure the delivery of your roadmap is more than just strokes on a canvas. This stage is about infusing tangible realities, each stroke representing a measurable outcome. Your strategic plans materialize into a vivid painting, linking P&L/BS Improvements to Valuation Gains with precision.

**6. Business Remodeling: Crafting the Future Landscape** Strategically dissect the existing business model, crafting a future landscape. It's not just about slicing and dicing; it's about sculpting a vision that transforms your business. Post-engagement, this Business Remodeling becomes the masterpiece, setting your corporate growth on an autopilot journey of adaptability and resilience.

**7. Knowledge Transfer: Empowering the Architectural Legacy** This final stroke guarantees active leadership involvement, creating an architectural legacy through knowledge transfer. It's not just about the end result; it's about empowering leadership teams to replicate transformative processes. The canvas becomes a living exhibit, showcasing a culture of continuous improvement and strategic agility.

# The Four Seasons Cycle of mOM

The mOM Methodology unfolds over a metaphorical one-year timeline, divided into four distinct phases or seasons:

**Phase 1: Autumn - Business Assessment and Opportunity Framing (Approximately 3 months)**

1. **Business Baseline: Unveiling the Canvas**

   - Undertake a comprehensive evaluation to reveal the current state of the business. Analyze its performance, capabilities, and potential areas for improvement.

2. **Opportunities Outline: Painting Future Perspectives**

   - Profile improvement opportunities, distinguishing between Quick Wins, Rapid Improvements, and Breakthroughs. Strategically frame the canvas, aligning resources with business objectives.

**Phase 2: Winter - Strategic Planning and Leadership Development (Approximately 3 months)**

3. **Value Flywheel: Brushing Momentum Into Strategy**
   - Develop a methodical plan to impart Momentum to business objectives. Craft deliberate strokes to form a masterpiece of immediate success and sustained growth.

4. **Executive Excellence: Sculpting Leadership Fortitude**

   - Sculpt leadership fortitude during this phase. Shape leaders capable of steering the business toward value-driven success, emphasizing the creation of integral sculptures of the organizational narrative.

**Phase 3: Spring - Execution and Tangible Outcomes (Approximately 3 months)**

5. **Value Delivery: Infusing Tangible Realities**

- Execute the strategic plan developed earlier. Infuse tangible realities into the canvas, with each stroke representing a measurable outcome. Materialize strategic plans into a vivid painting linked to financial improvements.

6. **Business Remodeling: Crafting the Future Landscape**

- Strategically dissect the existing business model and craft a future landscape. Sculpt a vision that transforms the business, setting it on an autopilot journey of adaptability and resilience.

**Phase 4: Summer - Knowledge Transfer and Continuous Improvement (Approximately 3 months)**

7. **Knowledge Transfer: Empowering the Architectural Legacy**
   - Ensure active leadership involvement in the final phase. Facilitate knowledge transfer to empower leadership teams to replicate transformative processes. The canvas becomes a living exhibit showcasing a culture of continuous improvement and strategic agility.

*Circularity: Assess – Evaluate - Repeat.*

This phased approach ensures a systematic progression through MOM, aligning with changing dynamics and facilitating informed decision-making at every step of the Value Creation Process. Whether led by OVC advisors r managed in-house by company or PE leadership teams, the process remains clear, standardized, and streamlined.

# Layer 2 - The Enablers

# Frameworks and Toolkits

# Merit-driven Operating Partner Playbook (mOPP)

mOPP is a vital toolkit of resources needed to streamline the mOM processes and help facilitate the interaction of Operating Partners with business counterparts and focal points.

**The mOPP is also referred to as The Merit-based Operating Partner Toolbox**

It is a combination of tools that cover various categories.

- Business Insights
- Cadence and Governance
- Rhythm and Leadership
- Innovation Drive
- Risk Management
- Forecasting
- Valuation

This section could be expanded into a full book on its own given the amount of details and potential exhibits and examples of tools it can cover. Instead, I shall aim to cover the key concepts and tools that any Operating Partner might need in order to best navigate a Value Creation Process. These tools are not intended to be a handicap but rather as streamlined task that an experienced OP can run auto-pilot mode and hence allow them to focus on more important value creation tasks. Again these are not cast in stone formats but rather open to adaptation and can be built on a mix-and-match basis. Also these are a non-exhaustive sample of a larger plethora of tools to apply and utilize.

# Rhythm and Cadence

The Meeting Scheduling Process. The OP needs to create rhythm early on through setting up weekly, monthly, quarterly meetings to cover various functions and assets in the organization.

Examples

SLT (Senior Leadership Team) meetings on weekly basis are extremely potent. Try to balance inclusivity with efficiency.

Monthly Strategy Sessions are also vital. Cover key strategic challenges and focus each month on solving one or two challenges. Carry over and check out as necessary.

Corporate-wide Innovation Forums on weekly basis are becoming popular. These should be risk free; give each staff member equal voice on these meeting; giving them a voice is half the win!

# Level 10 Methodology

Meetings should best follow the L10 methodology.

Level 10 Meetings emerge as a cornerstone of the Entrepreneurial Operating System (EOS). Crafted by Gino Wickman in his seminal work "Traction," these meetings drive a structured and transformative approach to team collaboration. Picture a setting where every participant, from leadership to frontlines, converges with utmost clarity and focus. The Level 10 Meeting is a weekly congregation designed to propel organizations forward by addressing key issues, fostering accountability, and ensuring strategic alignment. It's a carefully choreographed symphony where participants, much like a well-coordinated team, engage in a rhythm of reporting, analyzing, and resolving challenges. The beauty lies in its simplicity—a 90-minute session that cuts through the noise, allowing teams to concentrate on what truly matters. From scorecard reviews to identifying and solving obstacles, Level 10 Meetings embody the essence of efficiency and collaboration within the EOS framework. As teams gather around this strategic table, they're not just discussing; they're elevating their collective performance, steering the organization toward its goals with precision and cohesion.

# Meetings / Interview Guide

Treat  your meetings with OpCo staff with utmost care and respect. Be prepared! If you are not comfortable improvising and improvising well, then prepare an Interview or meeting guide with surgical precision questions that are purposeful and worthy of follow-up.

# Baselining Tools

To establish a proper assessment of the OpCo situation both qualitatively and quantitatively. Will focus more on the qualitative tools.

## SWOT Analysis

Some would consider this a cliché and passee as it is a basic tool taught at schools and universities; nonetheless, I found the dynamic it creates in any business ecosystem priceless. It brings out the true dynamics among staff and also the hidden and unspoken factual gems.   Sometime, staff are not comfortable talking about weaknesses as it could be very emotionally charges; no problem: drop the W!  SOT will do just fine; keep in mind what does not show up in Strengths is a Weakness; tomayto ... tomato.

# Planning Tools

To better plan what needs to be done and set priorities. These tools also are collaborative in nature and help  harmonize the strategy process between OpCo resources.

# VSEM Process

The VSEM stands out as one of the most powerful planning tools.

VSEM stands for Vision, Strategy, Execution, and Metrics. It is a framework that helps organizations to harmonize the strategy process between everyone who is involved in managing its deployment. The framework embodies four steps that help to define a clear path for the future:

1.      Vision: Identify where you want to end up. This is the long-term goal that everyone needs to clearly understand.

2.      Strategy: Define how you will achieve the above goal or goals. This can be the name of the strategy you are deploying as well as an outline of where resources will be used.

3.      Execution: Clearly state the way in which you will deploy your strategy. Identify and describe critical initiatives, programs, and actions to take that will support your strategy.

4.      Metrics: Acknowledge results and details into who is accountable for the execution of each step of the outlined plan. Measuring the outcome will keep you and your team on track.

The VSEM framework is a straightforward tool that encourages collaboration and simplifies the deployment process by using words that everyone understands and clearly knows. It is a useful tool for any organization looking to deploy a new strategy or improve their existing one.

# The Goal Alignment Tool

Set high goals and rally the troops. Work on both analytics and morale.

## The BHAG Approach

"...River Deep, Mountain High..."

*People with great goals are like majestic lion with manes, boldly standing out to both shock and inspire. Now, imagine yourself flaunting the most fabulous afro hairdo on a grand stage—radiating utmost confidence and singing your heart out. It does not matter if you might encounter stumbles, or face slips, but rest assured, you will not merely be noticed; you'll be engraved into memory. I say embrace the spirit of a Tina Turner – hustle, shine, whether in victory or defeat, for in the end, amidst the applause or the silence, they will always remember you... for your performance BHAGed them all!*

A BHAG, which stands for Big Hairy Audacious Goal, is like the superhero of business goals. Picture it as this grand, audacious mission that's so big and hairy that it's almost like trying to tame a lion. You know, not your everyday kind of goal; it's the stuff legends are made of.

Now, why is it so cool? Well, a BHAG is like the company's GPS, but instead of just giving directions, it's pointing towards the Everest of achievements. It's not your typical goal you hit and forget; it's the kind that transforms the whole vibe of the workplace. Think of it as a massive shot of inspiration that makes everyone jump out of bed, excited to conquer the day.

So, this big, audacious thing isn't just about hitting a target; it's about creating a buzz, sparking innovation, and turning a regular Tuesday into an epic quest. It's like telling your team, "Hey, we're not just here to play, we're here to change the game!" BHAGs make you dream big, push boundaries, and turn your company into a legend. It's not just a goal; it's an adventure waiting to happen!

And when you are done from your BHAG, BHAG another!

# Governance Tools

The basic tools to ensure all staff members are in line. The intention here is to avoid conflict and not to create one.

# Authority Matrix

An Authority Matrix, also known as a Responsibility Assignment Matrix (RAM) or RACI matrix, is a management tool that visually outlines the roles and responsibilities of individuals or teams within a project or organization. The matrix is particularly useful in clarifying who is accountable, responsible, consulted, and informed (hence the acronym RACI) for each task or decision.

The importance of an Authority Matrix lies in its ability to enhance clarity, efficiency, and accountability in the workplace. Here are key reasons why it is considered crucial:

1. **Clarity of Roles:** The matrix provides a clear and concise overview of who is responsible for what. This clarity helps prevent misunderstandings, reduces conflicts, and ensures that everyone knows their specific role in the project or process.

2. **Accountability:** By assigning specific roles and responsibilities, the matrix establishes accountability. Team members understand who is ultimately answerable for the success or completion of a task, which contributes to a more effective and accountable work environment.

3. **Communication:** The matrix serves as a communication tool, facilitating effective communication among team members. It

ensures that everyone involved is aware of their responsibilities and the roles of their colleagues, fostering a collaborative and communicative work environment.

4. **Efficiency:** With defined roles, tasks can be executed more efficiently. Team members know where to direct their efforts, reducing duplicated work and streamlining processes.

5. **Decision-Making:** The matrix clarifies who has the authority to make decisions on specific matters. This prevents delays caused by uncertainty about who should be involved in decision-making processes.

6. **Project Management:** In project management, the Authority Matrix helps project managers allocate resources effectively and ensures that critical tasks are not overlooked. It is a valuable tool for project planning and execution.

In summary, an Authority Matrix is a valuable tool for organizations and projects as it enhances role clarity, accountability, communication, and overall efficiency. It is particularly useful in complex projects or environments with multiple stakeholders, helping to navigate the intricacies of collaborative work.

# Table of Financial Authority (ToFA)

It is like an Authority Matrix but with focus on financial approval limits. It is best to combine both ToFA and AM in one document or tool.

# Risk Management Tools

Every OpCo needs to have its own internal risk management tools and processes. Ultimately a diligent OP owns the Risk Management and know how to share and escalate such sensitive information to the various constituents such as the Board, the PE sponsor, External Lenders, OpCo Leadership, Staff, etc..

## Risk Register

A Risk Register, also known as a Risk Log, is a systematic and organized document used in project management and business operations to identify, assess, monitor, and manage potential risks that could impact the successful execution of a project or the achievement of organizational objectives. It serves as a central repository for recording information about various risks, their potential impact, likelihood, and the strategies in place to mitigate or respond to them.

Key components typically found in a Risk Register include:

1. **Risk Identification:** A list of potential risks that could affect the project or business.

2. **Risk Description:** A detailed explanation of each identified risk, including its nature, source, and potential consequences.

3. **Risk Assessment:** An evaluation of the likelihood and impact of each risk on the project or business.

4. **Risk Owners:** Designated individuals or teams responsible for monitoring and addressing specific risks.

5. **Mitigation Strategies:** Planned actions to reduce the likelihood or impact of identified risks.

6. **Contingency Plans:** Pre-established measures to be implemented if a risk materializes.

7. **Status and Updates:** Regularly updated information on the status of each risk, including any changes in likelihood, impact, or mitigation efforts.

Maintaining a comprehensive Risk Register is imperative for proactive risk management. It equips teams and organizations with the foresight needed to anticipate potential challenges, make well-informed decisions, and allocate resources efficiently to address and mitigate risks throughout the entire project or business lifecycle. Exceptional Operating Partners (OPs) stand out by creating detailed and clear risk registers and implementing effective remedies.

This is akin a skilled captain who, rather than being the first to abandon ship, assesses the threat of sinking and orchestrates a coordinated response, ensuring that the situation is managed effectively with an "all-hands-on-deck" approach. The flip side of not knowing, is having an exodus of talent and resources, and it would be too late to remedy the crisis.

# 13 Week Cash Flow Projection

A 13-week cash flow projection is a financial forecast that outlines an organization's anticipated cash inflows and outflows over the next 13 weeks. This projection provides a short-term overview of the company's liquidity and helps in assessing its ability to meet financial obligations and operational needs. By detailing expected receipts from sources such as sales and investments, as well as outlining anticipated payments for expenses like salaries, utilities, and debt service, the 13-week cash flow projection enables businesses to proactively manage their cash position. This forecasting tool is valuable for identifying potential cash shortages or surpluses, allowing organizations to make informed decisions to optimize their financial stability in the near term.

# Banking Covenants Simulation

Many PE-backed OpCos are over-levered by design and by PE mandate to maximize Returns on Equity.

To that end, dealing with banking covenants is a continuous active process all OPs should be prepared to handle. By running Covenant Simulations, OPs are able to better anticipate any tricky situations ahead and remedy these before any escalation.

Projecting Funded EBITDA and Fixed Coverage Ratio (FCR) is a very potent financial assessments used to evaluate a company's compliance with the terms and conditions outlined in its banking covenants. Banking covenants are agreements between a borrower and a financial institution that establish specific financial metrics the borrower must maintain. Failure to meet these metrics may result in penalties or trigger default provisions.

1. **Funded EBITDA (Earnings Before Interest, Taxes, Depreciation, and Amortization):**

   - *Definition:* Funded EBITDA is a measure of a company's earnings that considers the impact of certain funded capital expenditures.

   - *Calculation:* It is typically calculated by adding back the funded portion of capital expenditures to the traditional EBITDA.

2. **Fixed Coverage Ratio (FCR):**

   - *Definition:* The Fixed Coverage Ratio is a financial metric that assesses a company's ability to cover its fixed charges (interest and principal payments) with its earnings.

   - *Calculation:* It is calculated by dividing the company's EBITDA by its fixed charges (interest and principal payments).

**Banking Covenant Simulation:**

- *Purpose:* These simulations involve projecting the financial metrics relevant to banking covenants to anticipate potential breaches or ensure compliance.

- *Process:* Companies use financial models and projections to simulate various scenarios, adjusting factors like EBITDA, capital expenditures, interest, and principal payments.

- *Risk Mitigation:* Simulations help identify potential covenant breaches early, allowing companies to take proactive measures to avoid default, such as negotiating with lenders, adjusting financial strategies, or securing additional funding.

**149**

By conducting these simulations, OPs can maintain a proactive approach to covenant compliance, ensuring financial stability and a healthy relationship with lenders.

# Tracking and Measurement Framework

As an integral part of a well-designed reporting system, OPs employ a comprehensive tracking and measurement approach across various facets of the OpCo operations. Examples below.

## Metrics / Performance Indicators

Non-Exhaustive examples below:

- *Revenue Analysis:*

    - Compare current period to the corresponding period in the prior year.

    - Monthly breakdown of overall revenue.

    - Adjust for initial-year seasonality.

- *EBITDA Analysis:*

    - Apply a similar construct as revenue analysis.

- *Specific Business KPI:*

    - Evaluate metrics such as Profit per X metric.

## Periodic Top-Down Dashboards

- CEO / Executive Leadership:
    - High-level financial overview.
    - Quarterly progress versus plan.

- o    Year-to-date progress versus plan.
- Operations:
  - o    More granular and robust.
  - o    Review company-specific KPIs.
  - o    Qualitative assessment with empirical insights.

# Portfolio Optimization and Periodization Process (POPP)

**Overview:**

Portfolio Optimization and Periodization Process (POPP) serves as a strategic prioritization framework within the broader Merit-driven Value Management System (mVMS) and the Merit-driven Operating Model (mOM). Specifically designed to optimize portfolios, POPP systematically rationalizes resource allocation through the lens of Operational Value Creation (OVC). As a result, it becomes a crucial indicator for Deal Teams in assessing whether to Hold, Grow, or Exit investments.

**Key Features:**

1. **Alignment with OVC Resources:**

    - POPP uniquely aligns with and leverages OVC resources, ensuring that portfolio optimization is intricately tied to the core principles of Operational Value Creation.

2. **Holistic Perspective:**

    - Integrated into the mVMS and mOM, POPP offers a holistic perspective on portfolio management. It considers not only financial metrics but also operational excellence and strategic alignment.

3. **Decision-Making Indicator:**

    - Acting as a decisive indicator for Deal Teams, POPP aids in making informed decisions regarding portfolio companies. It guides teams in determining whether to maintain current holdings, foster growth, or strategically exit investments.

4. **Importance of Operating Partners:**

- Recognizing the significance of Operating Partners in driving value creation, POPP emphasizes the crucial input of these partners. Their insights and contributions play a pivotal role in shaping the outcomes and decisions derived from the portfolio optimization process.

**Integration into Private Equity Ecosystem:** POPP plays a vital role in the private equity ecosystem, contributing to effective portfolio management and resource allocation. Incorporating the OVC perspective, it ensures a balanced and strategic approach, aligning with the overarching goals of value creation and sustainable growth.

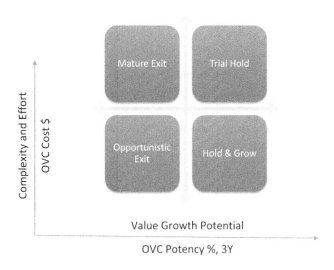

In essence, POPP is a dynamic framework that enhances the decision-making capabilities of Deal Teams, leveraging the principles of Operational Value Creation to optimize portfolios and foster success within the private equity landscape.

# Operating Partner Balanced ValueCard

The Operating Partner Balanced ValueCard is a strategic management tool that aligns with Total Value Creation (TVC) principles, providing a holistic framework for Operating Partners (OPs) to set targets and assess performance on a comprehensive basis. Drawing inspiration from TVC concepts, this tool focuses on balancing and optimizing key elements for value creation.

**Financial Perspective:**

*Value-Centric Cost Management:* Track costs related to value creation initiatives, ensuring efficient allocation of resources that directly contribute to maximizing shareholder value.

**Investomer Perspective:**

*Investomer Satisfaction Metrics:* Integrate value-related metrics, such as product/service impact and customer-perceived value and trade-offs with Investor gains and costs, into satisfaction measures. Assess the alignment of value creation propositions with customer expectations.

**Internal Process Perspective:**

*Process Efficiency and Value Enhancement:* Include measures of process efficiency and the effectiveness of value enhancement initiatives, emphasizing continuous improvement and the direct impact on shareholder value.

**Learning and Growth Perspective:**

*Employee Training for Value Creation:* Measure the effectiveness of training programs focused on value-centric management and improvement for employees, ensuring a skilled workforce capable of driving value.

**Strategic Objectives:**

*Value as a Core Strategic Pillar:* Explicitly state value creation as a core strategic objective, aligning it with overall business goals and emphasizing its pivotal role in the organization's success.

**Key Performance Indicators (KPIs):**

*Value-Related KPIs:* Develop specific KPIs related to value creation, such as the impact on shareholder returns, ROI for each OVC measure, and alignment with strategic objectives.

**Targets and Benchmarks:**

*Value Targets:* Set measurable targets for value improvement in products, services, and processes, ensuring that objectives directly contribute to maximizing overall value.

**Strategic Initiatives:**

*Value Enhancement Initiatives:* Highlight key initiatives aimed at enhancing product/service value and overall process efficiency, emphasizing the direct link between initiatives and increased shareholder value.

**Risk Management:**

*Value-Related Risks:* Assess and manage risks associated with potential value-related issues that may impact stakeholder satisfaction, financial performance, and overall stakeholder value.

**Communication and Alignment:**

*Value Awareness and Alignment:* Ensure that communication emphasizes the importance of value creation and aligns all employees with the organization's value objectives.

**Technology and Infrastructure:**

*Value Systems and Technology:* Evaluate the technology and infrastructure supporting value creation systems and ensure they facilitate continuous improvement and efficient value delivery.

**Stakeholder Engagement:**

*Value Impact on Stakeholders:* Communicate how value creation initiatives positively impact stakeholders, including customers, employees, and investors.

This integrated approach ensures that value creation is not only a consideration within processes but is the fundamental guiding principle throughout the organization's strategic objectives and performance measurement. The Balanced ValueCard encourages a culture of continuous improvement, investomer satisfaction, and financial viability, aligning with the TVC framework for sustained growth and success.

# Significance of the Balanced ValueCard (BVC)

*What does this mean?*

The Operating Partner's journey with the Balanced ValueCard (BVC) underscores a strategic imperative: all Operational Value Creation (OVC) measures must manifest a discernible impact on the overarching valuation of the organization. This pertinence becomes evident through both qualitative and quantitative Value Enhancement Measures (VEMs) which should ultimately be articulated in the company's financial statements—Profit and Loss (P&L), Cash Flow (CF), and Balance Sheet (BS).

Financial acumen is a prerequisite for Operating Partners as they decipher the ramifications of each alteration in these financial statements, essentially translating every change into tangible value. This aligns with the principle of steering towards "True North" – a trajectory that ensures sustained value creation.

Even when certain VEMs may not directly influence fundamental valuation metrics like Net Income or EBITDA, their impact on market sentiment, Valuation Multiples, and overall Go-To-Market readiness can be profound. Recognizing the nuanced interplay between these factors is pivotal, as it directly influences the organization's liquidity (exit routing) and market desirability.

A critical tenet of the BVC philosophy is rooted in the notion that if a Value Enhancement Measure fails to distinctly translate into a discernible value impact, it might warrant reconsideration for inclusion in the Value Management System (VMS) or as a focal point for the Operating Partner. In essence, the BVC serves as a compass, guiding the focus towards initiatives that demonstrably contribute to the enhancement of the organization's intrinsic value and market appeal.

# Scale and Scope Optimization Framework (SSOF)

## Managing Scale vs Scope Trade-offs

### A Key Skill for Operational Value Creation (OVC) Teams and Operating Partners (OP)

The SSOF is a strategic framework designed to empower OVC teams and OPs with the ability to assess growth opportunities effectively. It serves as a structured guide to swiftly identify and implement targeted approaches to enhance value. When presented with an opportunity, the OP utilizes the SSOF to suggest specific enhancement levers, clarifying whether the Value Enhancement Lever falls under Cost, Scope, Scale, or Optimize/(Re)Structure.

**Scale and Scope Optimization Framework**

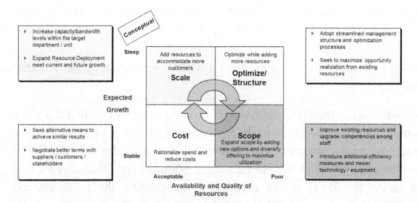

## Scale and Scope Optimization Framework

| | | |
|---|---|---|
| **Steep Growth** | **SCALE** *Add resources to accommodate more customers* Increase capacity/bandwidth levels within the target department/unit Enhance the ability to oversee increased demand and workload. Expand Resource Deployment to meet current and future growth Strategically allocate resources to align with present and anticipated growth. | **OPTIMIZE / (re) STRUCTURE** Optimize while adding more resources Adopt a streamlined management structure and optimization processes Streamline operational workflows and managerial processes. Seek to maximize opportunity realization from existing resources Enhance efficiency to derive maximum value from current resources. |
| **Stable Growth** | **COST** Rationalize spend and reduce costs Seek alternative means to achieve similar results Explore cost-effective alternatives to maintain desired outcomes. Negotiate better terms with suppliers/customers/stakeholders Optimize financial arrangements to reduce overall costs. | **SCOPE** Expand scope by adding new options and diversify offering to maximize utilization Improve existing resources and upgrade competencies among staff Invest in skill development and resource improvement. Introduce additional efficiency measures and newer technology/equipment Enhance capabilities through technological advancements. |
| | **High Resources** | **Limited Resources** |

**160**

For example, if faced with declining sales over the last two quarters, an OP cannot simply request an increase in sales. Understanding the reasons and implications is crucial. Moreover, if a business recently launched two production lines but sales haven't picked up, the implications become more drastic. The SSOF guides OPs to navigate such scenarios with strategic precision.

This framework is ideal for Logistics and Manufacturing Industry.

Other industries can be easily adapted by tweaking terms.

In Some specific industries, especially professional services, OP can selectively adapt new strategic lever focus areas to replace Optimize / (re) Structure such as:

| INNOVATE | ALIGN |
|---|---|
| *Embrace innovation for sustained growth* | *Align strategies with market demands* |
| Foster a culture of innovation within the organization | Regularly review and align business strategies with market trends |
|     Encourage employees to contribute innovative ideas. |     Conduct periodic market analyses to identify shifts in consumer behavior. |
|     Establish an innovation lab or platform for testing and implementing new concepts. |     Adjust business strategies to capitalize on emerging market opportunities. |
| Explore new market trends and emerging technologies | Diversify product or service offerings to meet changing demands |
|     Stay informed about industry advancements to identify growth opportunities. |     Evaluate the portfolio and introduce new offerings based on market demand. |
|     Invest in research and development to stay ahead of the competition. |     Leverage customer feedback to tailor products/services to evolving preferences. |

# Value Engine Flywheel (VEF)

**Overview:**

The Value Engine Flywheel (VEF) is a dynamic and integral component that seamlessly aligns with the broader Total Value Creation (TVC) framework. It operates as a versatile "mix and match" laundry list, comprising a constantly evolving set of value enhancement levers. These levers serve as the fundamental building blocks for crafting detailed Value Creation Plans or Investment Theses in pre-acquisition scenarios.

**Collaborative and Modular Approach:**

VEF is designed to be both collaborative and modular. It offers a plethora of value creation options, recognizing that each business scenario requires a tailored and adaptable approach. Operating Partners play a pivotal role in this process, employing their expertise to strategically choose, prioritize, and allocate resources effectively.

**Strategic Decision-Making:**

Much like a skilled builder with a set of Lego blocks, Operating Partners leverage VEF to make strategic decisions. It's not merely about identifying what needs to be done, but also about the "when," "by whom," and "at what cost." The key lies in the ability to envision the optimal structure and methodically craft it with precision, using the fewest blocks in the most efficient manner.

**Crafting Optimal Value Engines:**

Operating Partners function as visionary builders, meticulously selecting and combining the right levers from the VEF toolkit. Similar to constructing with Lego blocks, the emphasis is on building the most efficient and effective structure. While anyone can eventually figure out how to build higher and larger Lego structures, only a select few can create that truly optimal structure worthy of being displayed on the mantle.

In essence, VEF empowers Operating Partners to navigate the complexities of value creation, providing them with a dynamic set of tools to craft bespoke solutions that drive success in both detailed Value Creation Plans and pre-acquisition strategies.

# Example of a VEF Delivery Process

Typically a OVC initiatives lead by additional resources or external OPs should have a minimum ROI of 10x.

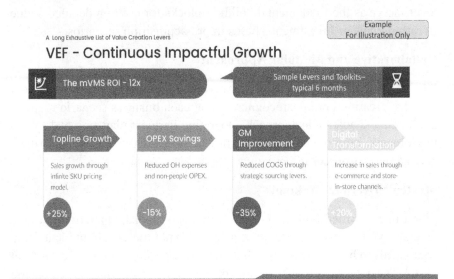

# The Tech-Savvy Operating Partner's 20/20 Augmented Vision

For the tech-savvy PE and OPs, technology from Industry 4.0 realms offers a tremendous advantage to augment their scope of tools.

1. **Value and Margin Optimization:**

   - **WC Optimization (Year 1 to 3 window):**

     - Implement advanced predictive analytics for efficient working capital optimization.

     - Explore blockchain-based smart contracts for automated payment cycles.

   - **JIT / Build to Order:**

     - Integrate AI for demand forecasting in JIT manufacturing.

     - Utilize IoT for real-time tracking in build-to-order processes.

   - **Strategic Sourcing:**

     - Employ AI algorithms for dynamic sourcing strategies based on market conditions.

     - Utilize blockchain for transparent and secure supplier relationships.

2. **Product / Portfolio Optimization:**

   - **SKU Analysis Standardization:**

     - Implement AI algorithms for continuous SKU performance monitoring.

     - Optimize supply chains through IoT-enabled SKU tracking.

**164**

- **Profitability per SKU:**

  - Utilize machine learning for dynamic pricing optimization at the SKU level.

  - Employ predictive analytics for SKU demand forecasting.

- **Pricing Model:**

  - Implement subscription-based pricing models for recurring revenue.

  - Introduce dynamic bundling based on customer behavior analytics.

3. **Balanced Sourcing:**

   - **Global Sourcing Strategy:**

     - Implement AI-driven global sourcing strategies based on geopolitical and economic factors.

     - Utilize blockchain for transparent and secure global sourcing transactions.

   - **Local Sourcing Initiatives:**

     - Explore AI for assessing the viability of local sourcing initiatives.

     - Integrate blockchain for transparent and traceable local sourcing practices.

   - **Risk Mitigation in Sourcing:**

     - Implement AI algorithms for real-time risk assessment in the sourcing process.

     - Utilize blockchain for transparent risk mitigation plans.

4. **Business Model Realignment / Pivot:**

   - **Online Strategy:**

**165**

- Explore AI-driven personalization for online customer experiences.
- Integrate AR/VR technologies for virtual product trials and immersive shopping.

- **Store in Store:**
  - Innovate store layouts with AI-driven customer flow analytics.
  - Introduce interactive kiosks for in-store product exploration.

- **Loyalty (Pay to Play):**
  - Implement blockchain-based loyalty programs for enhanced security.
  - Utilize machine learning for predictive loyalty program enhancements.

- **Negative WC:**
  - Implement blockchain-based supply chain transparency for efficient working capital management.
  - Introduce smart contracts to automate payment processes.

- **Cost + to Value-Add (Differentiation):**
  - Leverage IoT for real-time product tracking to justify premium pricing.
  - Introduce sustainability initiatives as a value-added component.

5. **Add-on and Bolt-on Acquisition:**
   - **Platform Play:**

- Explore acquisitions with integrated AI capabilities for seamless platform transitions.

- Utilize blockchain for secure data integration during acquisitions.

- **Bridge Plays:**

  - Integrate machine learning for predictive analysis of potential acquisition synergies.

  - Explore IoT for rapid integration of acquired technologies.

6. **Leveraging (Plain Vanilla) and Deleveraging (LBO):**

   - **Evaluate Leveraging Options:**

     - Use AI for comprehensive risk assessments in leveraging decisions.

     - Explore blockchain for transparent tracking of leveraged investments.

   - **Deleveraging (LBO):**

     - Implement AI-driven simulations for optimal deleveraging strategies.

     - Utilize blockchain for transparent communication with stakeholders during LBOs.

7. **Cost and Capital Rationalization:**

   - **Asset Stripping:**

     - Use machine learning algorithms for predictive asset performance assessment.

     - Explore blockchain-based asset tokenization for liquidity.

   - **Strategic Focus:**

**167**

- Utilize data analytics for strategic business unit alignment.

- Explore AI-driven business unit performance predictions.

8. **Competency and Team Scaling and Build-out:**

   - **C-Suite Hire:**

     - Utilize AI-driven talent acquisition tools for C-suite hires.

     - Introduce blockchain-based HR systems for secure executive data management.

   - **LTIP (RSU, Options, Phantom Shares, etc.) :**

     - Implement AI algorithms for predictive modeling of LTIP effectiveness.

     - Utilize blockchain for transparent and secure LTIP management.

   - **Fit for Purpose vs Designed for Growth:**

     - Utilize AI for workforce planning aligned with immediate needs and future growth.

     - Introduce blockchain for transparent organizational structure mapping.

   - **Profit Centers vs Cost Centers:**

     - Employ machine learning for dynamic categorization based on performance metrics.

     - Explore blockchain for transparent profit and cost center financials.

9. **Exit Preparation:**

   - **Institutionalization:**

**168**

- Implement AI-driven process documentation and standardization.

- Utilize blockchain for transparent and secure operational audits.

- **IPO Readiness:**

  - Use machine learning for predictive IPO readiness assessments.

  - Explore blockchain for transparent financial reporting and compliance.

- **ERP (not a PE priority):**

  - Implement AI for dynamic ERP prioritization based on evolving business needs.

  - Utilize blockchain for transparent ERP system data management.

10. **Outsourcing:**

- **Strategic Outsourcing Partnerships:**

  - Leverage AI for identifying and evaluating strategic outsourcing partners.

  - Implement blockchain for secure and transparent communication in outsourcing agreements.

- **Cost-Benefit Analysis:**

  - Utilize advanced analytics for comprehensive cost-benefit analyses.

  - Implement machine learning for predictive cost assessments in outsourcing decisions.

- **Quality Assurance in Outsourcing:**

  - Employ IoT for real-time quality monitoring in outsourced processes.

**169**

- Utilize blockchain for transparent and traceable quality assurance records.

11. **Strategic Partnerships and Alliances:**

- **Industry Collaborations:**
    - Employ AI for identifying potential collaborators within the industry.
    - Utilize blockchain for secure data sharing in collaborative projects.

- **Cross-Industry Alliances:**
    - Implement machine learning for identifying synergies with complementary industries.
    - Utilize blockchain for secure and transparent cross-industry data exchanges.

- **Innovative Ecosystem Partnerships:**
    - Leverage AI for identifying and joining innovative ecosystems.
    - Implement blockchain for secure and traceable transactions within ecosystems.

12. **Customer-Centric Initiatives:**

- **Customer Experience Enhancement:**
    - Utilize AI for predictive modeling of customer preferences.
    - Implement blockchain for secure and transparent customer feedback management.

- **Personalization Tactics:**
    - Employ machine learning algorithms for real-time personalization.
    - Utilize blockchain for secure and traceable personalized offers.

- **Feedback Loops:**

- Implement IoT for real-time feedback data collection.

- Utilize blockchain for secure and transparent feedback loop management.

13. **Business Innovation:**

- **Corporate Venture Capital Approach:**

   - Implement AI-driven screening processes for potential ventures.

   - Utilize blockchain for transparent investment tracking and management.

- **Technology Transformation:**

   - Explore partnerships with start-ups for early access to emerging technologies.

   - Implement AI-driven innovation workshops for internal ideation.

14. **Digital Transformation:**

- **Digital Infrastructure Investment:**

   - Utilize AI for predicting digital infrastructure needs based on business growth.

   - Implement blockchain for secure and transparent digital asset management.

- **Data-Driven Decision-Making:**

   - Promote the use of machine learning for data-driven decision-making.

   - Utilize blockchain for transparent data lineage and integrity.

- **Automation and AI Integration:**

   - Explore IoT for automation in operational processes.

**171**

- Leverage blockchain for secure and transparent integration of AI and automation.

15. **Environmental, Social, and Governance (ESG) Initiatives:**

- **Sustainable Practices:**
  - Utilize AI for optimizing sustainable business practices.
  - Implement blockchain for transparent and traceable sustainability reporting.

- **Social Responsibility Programs:**
  - Employ machine learning for assessing the impact of social responsibility programs.
  - Utilize blockchain for secure and transparent management of social responsibility initiatives.

- **Governance Framework Enhancement:**
  - Implement AI for predictive modeling of governance framework effectiveness.
  - Utilize blockchain for secure and transparent governance documentation.

16. **Market Expansion Strategies:**

- **Geographical Diversification:**
  - Utilize AI for market analysis to identify optimal geographical diversification opportunities.
  - Implement blockchain for secure and transparent cross-border transactions.

- **New Product/Service Markets:**
  - Employ machine learning to identify innovative products or services.

**172**

- Utilize blockchain for secure and transparent new product/service launches.

- **Strategic Alliances for Market Entry:**

  - Utilize AI for predicting the success of strategic alliances in new markets.

  - Implement blockchain for secure and transparent data sharing within alliances.

17. **Technology Integration for Efficiency:**

- **Cloud Computing Adoption:**

  - Explore AI for optimizing cloud resource allocation.

  - Leverage blockchain for secure and transparent cloud service transactions.

- **Integration of IoT Devices:**

  - Implement AI for optimizing IoT device integration.

  - Utilize blockchain for secure and transparent IoT data transactions.

- **Blockchain Applications:**

  - Explore AI for identifying innovative applications of blockchain technology.

  - Implement blockchain for secure and transparent business transactions.

18. **Talent Development and Retention:**

- **Leadership Development Programs:**

  - Utilize AI for personalized leadership development plans.

  - Employ blockchain for secure and transparent tracking of leadership development milestones.

- **Employee Engagement Initiatives:**

**173**

- Implement machine learning for predicting effective employee engagement strategies.
- Utilize blockchain for transparent and traceable employee feedback management.

- **Competitive Compensation Models:**
    - Employ AI for predictive modeling of competitive compensation structures.
    - Implement blockchain for secure and transparent compensation transactions.

19. **Regulatory Compliance and Risk Management:**

- **Comprehensive Compliance Framework:**
    - Utilize AI for continuous monitoring of regulatory compliance.
    - Implement blockchain for secure and transparent compliance documentation.

- **Risk Assessment and Mitigation:**
    - Employ machine learning for real-time risk assessment.
    - Utilize blockchain for transparent and traceable risk mitigation plans.

- **Crisis Management Protocols:**
    - Explore AI for predicting potential crisis scenarios.
    - Implement blockchain for secure and transparent crisis management documentation.

20. **Production and Manufacturing Excellence:**

- **Manufacturing Process Optimization:**
    - Utilize AI for predictive maintenance to minimize equipment downtime.

- Implement IoT sensors for real-time monitoring of manufacturing processes.

- **Supply Chain Integration:**

  - Employ machine learning for demand forecasting to optimize inventory levels.

  - Utilize blockchain for transparent and traceable supply chain transactions.

  - Lean Manufacturing

Again these levers are just a sample and by no means make an exhaustive list. OPs can pick and choose at will.

# The Traditional Menu – A La Carte Value Creation Levers

For a more traditional approach of mix and match of tools and levers, many options can be used to brainstorm solutions and fill the blanks.

**"The Cheat Sheet": OVC Brick & Mortar LEGO Blocks**

| Revenue-Building Levers | EBITDA-Growth Levers | Cost-Reduction Levers | Other Levers |
|---|---|---|---|
| Market Expansion | Cost Synergies | Administrative Efficiency | Leadership Development |
| Product Innovation | Operational Efficiency | Overhead Reduction | Board Governance |
| Pricing Optimization | Technology Integration | Cost Benchmarking | Shareholder Reporting |
| Sales Excellence | Process Optimization | Vendor Management | LP Relations |
| Customer Loyalty | Lean Operations | Travel Expense Control | Exit Strategies |
| New Markets Entry | Supply Chain Resilience | Utility Cost Management | Capital Allocation |
| Service Innovation | Scalable Platforms | Lean Manufacturing | Debt Management |
| Brand Enhancement | Agile Workforce | Material Procurement | Strategic Planning |
| Channel Optimization | Talent Retention | Process Redesign | M&A Integration |
| Digital Presence | Operational Excellence | Design Optimization | Portfolio Diversification |
| Strategic Alliances | Procurement Efficiency | Facility Rationalization | Strategic Alliances |

176

| | | | |
|---|---|---|---|
| Emerging Markets | Labor Productivity | Energy Cost Reduction | Risk Mitigation |
| Niche Segmentation | IT Infrastructure | Inventory Optimization | Financial Engineering |
| Brand Positioning | Automation Strategies | IT Cost Management | Investor Relations |
| Cross-Sell Synergies | Capex Optimization | Capex Control | Data Security |
| Upselling Strategies | Robotic Process Automation | IT Infrastructure | Regulatory Compliance |
| Targeted Marketing | Manufacturing Excellence | Facility Consolidation | Crisis Management |
| E-commerce Growth | Workforce Training | Telecommuting Adoption | Corporate Culture |
| Customer Retention | Continuous Improvement | Sustainable Practices | Employee Engagement |
| Product Differentiation | Asset Utilization | Digital Transformation | Succession Planning |
| Revenue Diversification | Digital Workflows | Cloud Computing | Digital Literacy |
| Subscription Models | Data-driven Operations | Robotic Process Automation | Blockchain Adoption |
| Data Monetization | AI-driven Analytics | Shared Services | Corporate Citizenship |
| Geographic Expansion | Predictive Maintenance | Smart Technologies | Corporate Social Responsibility |
| Innovation Hubs | Quality Assurance | Outsourcing Efficiencies | Environmental Stewardship |
| Customer Experience | Inventory Management | Offshoring Benefits | Community Engagement |

| Brand Recognition | Cost Allocation | Streamlined Procurement | Knowledge Management |
|---|---|---|---|
| Strategic Partnerships | Outsourcing Synergies | Waste Reduction | Innovation Culture |
| Value-Added Services | Variable Cost Control | Technology Rationalization | Brand Equity |
| Market Intelligence | Supplier Negotiation | Automated Workflows | ESG Compliance |
| Sales Force Optimization | Resource Optimization | Operational Streamlining | Stakeholder Engagement |
| Product Portfolio | Strategic Sourcing | SaaS Adoption | Board Diversity |
| Pricing Models | Regulatory Compliance | Paperless Operations | Sustainable Investments |
| Agile Marketing | Risk Management | Green Initiatives | Legal Compliance |
| Influencer Collaborations | Crisis Preparedness | Energy Efficiency | Reputation Management |
| Brand Consistency | Debt Restructuring | Real Estate Optimization | Stakeholder Trust |
| Localized Offerings | Economies of Scale | Digital Expense Management | Data Security Governance |
| Omnichannel Strategy | Energy Optimization | Cybersecurity Efficiency | Crisis Communication |
| Customer Analytics | Facilities Management | AI-powered Analytics | Employee Advocacy |
| Digital Transformation | Infrastructure Upgrade | Digital Platforms | Talent Acquisition |
| Revenue Forecasting | Business Process Reengineering | Data Consolidation | Employee Well-being |

**178**

| AI-Driven Sales | Working Capital Efficiency | Electronic Documentation | Inclusive Hiring |
|---|---|---|---|
| Strategic Pricing | Shared Services | Agile Work Environments | Digital Ethics |
| Social Media Impact | Enterprise Resilience | Touchless Technologies | Thought Leadership |
| Global Market Entry | Value Engineering | Virtual Collaboration | Industry Advocacy |
| Personalized Offers | Intellectual Property | Remote Work Solutions | Customer Education |
| Mobile Optimization | Digital Adoption | Green Initiatives | Employee Training |
| Customer Journey | Cloud Integration | Energy Efficiency | Digital Culture |
| Ecosystem Integration | Agile Supply Chains | Real Estate Optimization | Blockchain Adoption |
| Personalized Offers | Intellectual Property | Remote Work Solutions | Customer Education |

This remains a non-exhaustive list.

**179**

# Technology-Inspired Value Creation Levers

For the Tech Savvy Operating Partner, another set of fancy blocks could be used.

| Crypto Payment Solutions | Cybersecurity Automation Measures | Automated Administrative Processes | Strategic Portfolio Optimization |
|---|---|---|---|
| AI-Enhanced Upselling | Data Privacy Compliance Framework | Telecommuting Efficiency Tech | Governance Framework Enhancement |
| Blockchain in Loyalty Programs | Resilient Digital Supply Chains | Sustainable Procurement Innovations | Shareholder Value Communication |
| Sustainable Packaging Innovations | Smart Manufacturing Technologies | Digital Transformation for Cost Control | LP Reporting Automation |
| Influencer Marketing ROI Analysis | AI-Enhanced Predictive Maintenance | Blockchain in Invoice Verification | Exit Strategy Optimization |
| Predictive Analytics in Sales | Blockchain for Quality Assurance | Green Office Technologies | Capital Structure Rationalization |
| Voice Commerce Optimization | Cloud-Based Financial Planning | Eco-Friendly Travel Technologies | AR/VR Product Trials |
| Personalized Subscription Models | Agile Procurement Decision Support | AI-Enhanced Cost Benchmarking | Regulatory Compliance Platforms |
| Virtual Reality in Customer Engage | Data-Driven Workforce Planning | IoT for Facilities Cost Optimization | Cybersecurity Governance |

| | | | |
|---|---|---|---|
| E-commerce Fulfillment Efficiency | Sustainable Energy Procurement | Paperless Operations Technologies | Crisis Communication Protocols |
| Sustainable Supply Chain Collab | Predictive Analytics in Facilities | Sustainable IT Infrastructure | Talent Management Frameworks |
| Digital Wallet Integration | Blockchain for Transparent Compliance | Automated Workflow Solutions | Leadership Succession Planning |
| Social Media Listening Strategies | Agile Capex Planning | Digital Culture Adoption Platforms | Customer Retention Analytics |
| Customer Journey Optimization | Sustainable Technology Adoption | Touchless Office Technologies | Innovation Culture Promotion |
| AI-Driven Product Recommendations | AI in Crisis Simulation Protocols | Remote Work Technology Solutions | Digital Literacy Initiatives |
| Augmented Reality Shopping Exp | Cybersecurity Governance Models | Green Office Initiatives | Blockchain Governance Models |
| Customer Data Monetization | Predictive Talent Analytics | Electronic Documentation Platforms | Corporate Social Responsibility |
| Agile Supply Chain Integration | Leadership Development Platforms | Sustainable IT Infrastructure | Environmental Stewardship Initiatives |
| Subscription-Based Marketplaces | Virtual Leadership Training | Cloud-Based Collaboration Efficiency | Community Engagement Platforms |
| Personalized Loyalty Programs | Employee Wellness Analytics | Digital Culture Promotion Platforms | ESG Reporting Platforms |
| Mobile App Gamification | Sustainable IT Infrastructure | Touchless Office Technologies | Knowledge Management Systems |
| Dynamic Pricing Algorithms | Cloud-Based Collaboration Platforms | Remote Work Technology Solutions | IP Protection Strategies |
| Cross-Border E-commerce Strategies | Touchless Office Technologies | Green Office Initiatives | Brand Reputation Management |

| | | | |
|---|---|---|---|
| Social Media Community Building | Remote Work Technology Solutions | Electronic Documentation Platforms | Stakeholder Engagement Platforms |
| Hyper-Personalized Marketing | Green Office Initiatives | Sustainable IT Infrastructure | Financial Engineering Solutions |
| AI-Enhanced Predictive Sales | Electronic Documentation Platforms | Predictive Analytics for Cybersecurity | Investor Relations Platforms |
| Blockchain for Transparent Pricing | Sustainable IT Infrastructure | Lean Operations in Manufacturing | Data Security Governance |
| Mobile Payment Innovations | Predictive Analytics for Facilities | Energy-Efficient Manufacturing | Crisis Simulation Platforms |
| Data-Driven Cross-Sell Strategies | Blockchain for Employee Records | Sustainable Packaging Automation | Employee Advocacy Initiatives |
| Collaborative Marketing Campaigns | AI in Talent Acquisition | Predictive Analytics for Procurement | Talent Acquisition Technologies |
| AI-Driven Geo-targeting | Machine Learning in Employee Training | AI-Enhanced Robotic Automation | Employee Well-being Platforms |
| Sustainable E-commerce Practices | Blockchain for Transparent Compensation | Blockchain in Supply Chain Transactions | Inclusive Hiring Initiatives |
| Chatbot-Enhanced Customer Support | Sustainable Office Practices | Predictive Analytics for Tax Planning | Sustainable Procurement Platforms |
| Gamified Customer Feedback Systems | Predictive Analytics for Cybersecurity | Sustainable Technologies Adoption | Circular Supply Chain Adoption |
| AI-Optimized Email Marketing | Lean Operations Implementation | Energy-Efficient IT Infrastructure | |
| Blockchain for Supply Chain Visibility | Energy-Efficient Manufacturing | Digital Process Reengineering | |

| Predictive Analytics for Inventory | Sustainable Packaging Solutions | Smart Office Technologies | |
|---|---|---|---|
| Social Media Influencer Partnerships | IoT in Cost-Effective Operations | | |

### 2040 Prediction:

*More of the techy value creation levers shall be adopted and to some extent the traditional grey-haired OP shall be substituted by a younger more tech-agile player.*

# The OPEO Driving the mVMS

The OP as an Executive Officer can take lead on driving the mVMS through a PMO (Project Management Office) approach .

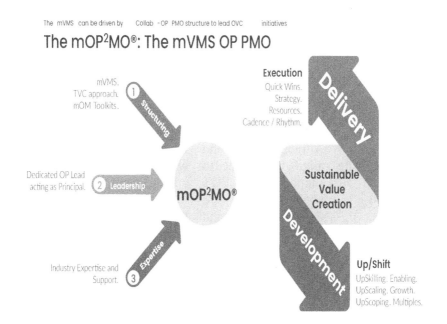

The mVMS can be driven by    Collab - OP PMO structure to lead OVC    initiatives

## The mOP²MO®: The mVMS OP PMO

mVMS.
TVC approach.
mOM Toolkits.

**(1) Structuring**

Dedicated OP Lead acting as Principal.

**(2) Leadership**

**mOP²MO®**

Industry Expertise and Support.

**(3) Expertise**

**Execution**
Quick Wins.
Strategy.
Resources.
Cadence / Rhythm.

**Delivery**

**Sustainable Value Creation**

**Development**

**Up/Shift**
UpSkilling. Enabling.
UpScaling. Growth.
UpScoping. Multiples.

# The Merit-driven Value Accelerator (mVA)

This is a blitz approach to value creation when a PE firm or sponsor is short on resources, or on a pressed timeline, or the Operating has limited bandwidth.

This is akin to "if you had to memorise all of the mVMS elements but could not! Is there a Cheat Sheet?"

| Key Element | Objective | Execution |
|---|---|---|
| **Talent Synergy: The Value Coach(es)** | Attract, nurture, and align top talent to support the CEO's vision. | Build a high-performing team with diverse skills, emphasizing collaboration, innovation, and adaptability. |
| **Rapid Baseline Establishment** | Quickly understand and diagnose key challenges and opportunities. | Utilize proven methodologies to expedite the assessment of the current state, identifying critical areas for improvement. |
| **Quick Wins Identification: Low Hanging Fruits** | Swiftly pinpoint and execute on opportunities that yield immediate positive impact. | Implement agile processes to identify and prioritize low-hanging fruits, fostering a culture of continuous improvement. |
| **BHAG Early Adoption and Makeover** | Set ambitious long-term goals to inspire and guide strategic decisions. | Define and communicate a compelling Big Hairy Audacious Goal (BHAG) early, nurturing it through continuous refinement. |
| **Structured Frameworks and Collaboration System** | Establish a structured approach and collaborative environment for | Implement a proven framework, fostering transparent communication and cross-functional collaboration. |

| | | |
|---|---|---|
| | efficient decision-making. | |
| **Incentive Alignment: Balancing Gain and Pain** | Motivate teams through well-aligned incentives, considering both rewards and consequences. | Design a balanced incentive system that encourages desired behaviors, linking personal and organizational success. |
| **Advisory Network Engagement** | Leverage external expertise for industry insights and financial acumen. | Assemble and engage a network of accessible advisors, incorporating specialized knowledge to inform strategic decisions. |
| **Task Force Empowerment** | Drive impactful initiatives through a dedicated task force of key starters and finishers. | Empower a task force with a clear mandate, fostering agility and accountability for successful project execution. |
| **Create a Rhythm Matrix Early** | Establish a regular cadence for effective communication and issue resolution. | Implement Level 10 (L10) meeting structures to ensure focused discussions, alignment on priorities, and swift issue resolution (Matrix: functional, asset-based). |

A Special Situation Blitz Tool to maximize value creation on 80/20 basis.

# The Merit-driven Value Accelerator ®

When a PE firm or sponsor is short on resources, on a pressed timeline, or the Operating Partner has limited bandwidth...

| mVA | Planning | Analysis | Delivery | 6-12 month Process |
|---|---|---|---|---|
| **Phase 1 Accelerated Support** | Talent Synergy Mapping | Rapid Baseline Establishment | Quick Wins Identification and Realization | |
| **Phase 2 Long Term Launch** | BHAG – Early Adoption and Makeover | Structured Frameworks and Collaborative System | Advisory Network Engagement | |
| **Phase 3 Enabling Support** | Incentive Alignment | Task Force Empowerment and Upskilling | Early Rhythm Matrices | |

# Evolution of Investment Paradigms

*"The Rise and Rise of the Principal Investor"*

*The line delineating PE and VC is becoming thinner; OPs will have to adapt to a more dynamic yet complex landscape of investment and value creation needs. This will eventually lead to a new OP profile; probably OP 4.0!*

## The Convergence of Private Equity and Venture Capital

### 1. Shifting Paradigms in Investment Dynamics

The traditional boundaries distinguishing Private Equity (PE) investments from Venture Capital (VC) startups are undergoing a significant transformation. The evolution of startups into mainstream corporations, characterized by a blend of their startup DNA and a VC mentality, challenges conventional narratives. This marks the inception of a new paradigm, fusing the influences of PE and VC in the contemporary investment landscape.

### 2. Rise of Principal Investors: Blurring Investment Boundaries

A surge in investors adopting the title of Principal Investors signifies a departure from the traditional compartmentalization of investment strategies. These investors, with diverse portfolios spanning early-stage VC ventures to mature PE stakes, operate with their Corporate Venture Capital (CVC) engines. This phenomenon, termed "The Rise and Rise of the Principal Investor," highlights a fluid and dynamic investment landscape as the dichotomy between PE and VC investments dissipates.

**188**

### 3. Corporate Venture Capital's Influence: Creating from Scratch

Contrary to the historical Add-on or Bolt-On approach of PE firms, Principal Investors leverage their in-house CVC engines to perpetually adopt a startup mindset. This shift has profound implications, allowing for continuous innovation, creation from scratch, and agility—a departure from the traditional buy-and-build model, highlighting the flexibility and adaptability associated with the VC world.

### 4. Pivotal Role of Operating Partners in the Evolving Landscape

As PE firms traditionally excel in the M&A terrain, the uncharted territories of startups and greenfield tech ventures pose unique challenges. The evolution of Operating Partners (OPs), traditionally sourced from deal teams or investment banking, becomes pivotal. The integration of VC skill sets within the OP team emerges as a compelling solution, emphasizing the need to equip OPs with an understanding of the startup cycle and navigate the intricacies of the tech-driven, greenfield landscape.

### 5. Venture Builder Studios: Catalysts for Enhanced Value Creation

The introduction of VC expertise within the OP team acts as a potent catalyst for enhanced value creation. Venture Builder Studios, functioning as shared service models or support umbrellas for OPs, prove invaluable. For some PE firms, the ability to establish of an in-house Venture Builder Studio aligns with this paradigm shift, aiming to empower clients by embedding VC capabilities within the traditional PE framework.

### 6. Symbiotic Integration for Multi-Faceted Advantages

The symbiotic integration of VC skill sets within the PE ecosystem yields multi-faceted advantages. OPs gain exposure to the dynamic startup culture, navigating greenfield terrains with finesse. Businesses, under the guidance of a hybrid OP team, benefit from dual expertise in deal-making and startup agility. Investors witness portfolios excelling in operational efficiency and thriving amidst the ever-changing technological disruption. This convergence of PE and VC skill sets within the OP framework emerges as a strategic imperative for those seeking not only to adapt but to thrive in the evolving landscape of modern investments.

# Industry 4.0 Challenges and Opportunities

## Unlocking Growth: Embracing Industry 4.0 in PE Portfolio Companies

In the era of Industry 4.0, characterized by the integration of Artificial Intelligence (AI) and Automation, adapting companies to this technological revolution is not merely a luxury but an imperative for sustained growth. This change in basic assumptions is fundamentally reshaping industries, and for Private Equity (PE) portfolio companies, embracing Industry 4.0 is a strategic necessity with profound implications for both growth and operational efficiencies, leading to substantial EBITDA improvements.

### Understanding Industry 4.0

Industry 4.0 represents the fourth industrial revolution, marked by the convergence of digital, physical, and biological technologies. At its core, it harnesses the power of AI and Automation to create smart, interconnected systems that can operate, communicate, and make decisions autonomously. This transformation extends across manufacturing, supply chains, and business processes, promising unprecedented levels of efficiency, flexibility, and innovation.

### Vitality for PE Portfolio Companies

For PE portfolio companies, the adoption of Industry 4.0 technologies is pivotal for unlocking growth opportunities and achieving operational excellence. Embracing AI and Automation translates into streamlined processes, reduced operational costs, and enhanced productivity—directly impacting EBITDA margins. The ability to respond swiftly to market dynamics and customer demands positions companies strategically for long-term success.

# Common Examples of AI and Automation Benefits

1. **Predictive Maintenance:** AI-driven predictive maintenance ensures machinery and equipment are serviced precisely when needed, minimizing downtime, and maximizing operational efficiency.

2. **Supply Chain Optimization:** Automation in supply chain processes, coupled with AI analytics, enables real-time monitoring, demand forecasting, and intelligent decision-making, ensuring optimal inventory levels and minimizing costs.

3. **Quality Control:** AI-powered image recognition and machine learning contribute to enhanced quality control, detecting defects with unprecedented accuracy and consistency.

4. **Customer Service Enhancement:** AI-driven chatbots and automation tools elevate customer service by providing instant responses, personalized interactions, and efficient query resolutions.

5. **Operational Streamlining:** Automation of routine tasks, from data entry to administrative processes, frees up human resources for more strategic, value-added activities.

# The OP's Role in Industry 4.0

Operating Partners (OPs) play a pivotal role in navigating PE portfolio companies through the Industry 4.0 landscape. Understanding AI and Automation is no longer a choice but a necessity for OPs, enabling them to identify opportunities for technology integration, assess risks, and drive strategic initiatives that harness the transformative potential of Industry 4.0. Equipping OPs with a comprehensive understanding of these technologies ensures they can lead portfolio companies towards not only surviving but thriving in the evolving digital era.

In conclusion, Industry 4.0 is a cornerstone for the future competitiveness of PE portfolio companies. Embracing AI and Automation is not just about staying current; it is the key to unlocking untapped potential, driving growth, and ensuring sustained relevance in an ever-evolving business landscape.

# Capturing the Opportunity: A PE Perspective

To effectively embrace and adapt to the challenges and opportunities presented by Industry 4.0, Private Equity (PE) firms can implement strategic initiatives that align with the transformative potential of emerging technologies. Here are key actions PE firms can take to better navigate the Industry 4.0 landscape in their portfolio companies (OpCos):

**1. Prioritize Digital Due Diligence:** Incorporate digital due diligence as a crucial step in the pre-acquisition process. Evaluate a target company's digital capabilities, technological infrastructure, and preparedness for Industry 4.0. This enables PE firms to make well-informed investment decisions and assess the OpCo's readiness for digital transformation.

**2. Actively Drive Technology Integration:** Post-acquisition, take an active role in integrating Industry 4.0 technologies into OpCos. Implement AI-driven analytics, automation solutions, and Internet of Things (IoT) devices to optimize operational processes, boost productivity, and achieve cost efficiencies.

**3. Invest in Talent Development:** Recognize the pivotal role of human capital in digital transformation. Invest in talent development programs within OpCos, upskilling existing employees to collaborate effectively with new technologies. Additionally, recruit specialized professionals with expertise in AI, data analytics, and other Industry 4.0 domains.

**4. Champion Operational Excellence Initiatives:** Leverage Industry 4.0 to drive operational excellence within OpCos. Implement smart manufacturing practices, predictive maintenance, and supply chain optimization to enhance overall efficiency and reduce operational costs.

**5. Establish Innovation Hubs and Centers of Excellence:** Foster a culture of innovation by establishing innovation hubs or centers of excellence dedicated to driving technological advancements within OpCos. These hubs can serve as testing grounds for emerging technologies and incubators for innovative ideas.

**6. Facilitate Collaborations and Partnerships:** Encourage collaborations and partnerships between OpCos and technology providers, startups, or industry peers. Facilitate access to cutting-edge technologies, industry trends, and innovative solutions through strategic partnerships.

**7. Strategically Pursue Add-on Acquisitions:** Continue the traditional PE approach of add-on acquisitions with a focus on strategically acquiring technology-focused companies. These acquisitions can accelerate OpCos' digital capabilities and contribute to their journey toward Industry 4.0.

**8. Prioritize Cybersecurity Measures:** Acknowledge the increased importance of cybersecurity in the digital era. Prioritize and implement robust cybersecurity measures within OpCos to safeguard against potential cyber threats, ensuring the security and integrity of digital assets.

By proactively adopting these measures, PE firms can position their OpCos to thrive in the evolving landscape of Industry 4.0. Aligning technology initiatives with overarching business objectives will contribute to the overall competitiveness, resilience, and long-term success of portfolio companies in the digital age.

# The Imperative for OP 4.0!

*"When Friends meets The Big Bang Theory."*

## Navigating the Digital Transformation

In the age of rapid technological advancement, Operating Partners (OPs) are undergoing a transformative shift, entering what we term "OP 4.0." Beyond adapting to Industry 4.0, OPs are emerging as key drivers, utilizing their expertise to catalyze transformation within portfolio companies. This evolution involves more than embracing digital transformation; it signifies a shift in mindset toward constant evolution, mirroring the dynamic technologies reshaping industries.

As change catalysts, OPs in the realm of OP 4.0 function as navigators, steering the integration of digital technologies with operational excellence. It goes beyond introducing the latest technologies; it's about seamlessly aligning digital integration with operational strategies. Visualize an OP as a technological expert, blending traditional operational methodologies with the transformative potential of Industry 4.0. This demands more than surface-level understanding; it requires deep exploration into artificial intelligence, automation, and interconnected systems.

At the forefront of OP 4.0, these professionals wear the dual hats of strategist and technologist. They actively shape technology-driven decisions, aligning courses with overarching business strategies. Picture an OP as a techno-strategist, navigating the complex digital landscape with the precision of a seasoned captain. It's not about embracing technology for its own sake; it's about strategically selecting and integrating digital tools that resonate with the unique needs of each portfolio company.

Implementation, another facet of OP 4.0, involves a delicate dance of technological adoption. It's more than rolling out new software or hardware; it's about fostering a tech-savvy culture throughout the portfolio company. Here, the OP is an artisan, sculpting an environment where every employee is not just a user but an empowered contributor to the digital evolution. Envision an OpCo where the implementation of cutting-edge technology is not met with resistance but embraced as an opportunity for growth and advancement.

Knowledge transfer and mentorship become the core of OP 4.0. These professionals go beyond being bearers of knowledge; they become architects of a learning ecosystem. Visualize an OP as a digital sage, instilling a culture of continuous learning and innovation within OpCos. Through mentorship programs, they pass on the torch of technological acumen, ensuring that the entire workforce becomes not just proficient but enthusiastic contributors to the digital transformation.

In the era of Industry 4.0, OPs are the drivers, playing a crucial role in orchestrating technological integration, operational efficiency, and cultural transformation. The need for OP 4.0 is not merely a response to change; it's a commitment to lead the charge in shaping the future of operational excellence amid the age of digital disruption.


Operating Partners (OPs) require continuous training on the latest advancements and applications of artificial intelligence (AI). This ongoing education is essential to ensure that OPs stay abreast of the rapidly evolving landscape of AI technologies and understand their diverse applications across various industries. Given the transformative impact of AI on business operations, strategic decision-making, and overall industry dynamics, regular training equips OPs with the knowledge and skills necessary to effectively leverage AI for enhanced value creation within portfolio companies. By staying current on AI advancements, OPs can proactively identify opportunities, navigate challenges, and contribute meaningfully to the successful integration of AI technologies into the operational fabric of their respective organizations.


The next section admits that OP 4.0 are made and not found. Training and coaching are a must to furnish such skillsets inhouse as opposed to hire external Digital Transformation catalysts.

# Coaching and Training OPs on Industry 4.0 and Venture Building

The following coaching and training plans are important to cover in any PE firm planning to augment its inhouse OVC skillset:

1) Industry 4.0 Capabilities

2) Venture Building Skills

# The Need for Industry 4.0 Coaching for OPs

Industry 4.0: Opportunities and Risks

PE firms need to provide a comprehensive training program focused on the adoption and risks associated with Industry 4.0 to their OPs. In response to the rapidly changing technological landscape, our training initiative is designed to empower professionals with the knowledge and skills required to navigate the complexities of Industry 4.0 effectively. Such a program would cover a broad spectrum of topics, ensuring a holistic understanding of the various facets of digital transformation within the context of Industry 4.0.

A suitable training curriculum begins by offering a foundational understanding of Industry 4.0, delving into the core principles, technologies, and the transformative impact it brings to businesses. Participants gain insights into the integration of artificial intelligence, automation, data analytics, and the Internet of Things (IoT) into operational processes.

One key focus of such training is the identification and assessment of risks associated with Industry 4.0 adoption. Seeking in-depth insights into potential challenges and pitfalls, equipping participants with the skills to proactively manage and mitigate risks. This would include a thorough exploration of cybersecurity considerations, data privacy concerns, and the implications of interconnected systems on overall operational resilience.

Customized training initiatives should stand out for their practical approach, incorporating real-world case studies and scenarios. Participants engage in hands-on exercises and simulations that simulate Industry 4.0 challenges, allowing them to apply theoretical knowledge to practical situations. This experiential learning approach enhances the effectiveness of the training, ensuring that participants are not only knowledgeable but also adept at applying their insights in real-world scenarios.

Furthermore, such a training program emphasizes the importance of continuous learning and adaptability in the face of evolving technological landscapes. It is more about providing resources for staying current with the latest Industry 4.0 trends and advancements, enabling OP professionals to remain agile and responsive to industry changes.

It is safe to say, a comprehensive Industry 4.0 adoption and risks training program serves as a valuable resource for professionals seeking to navigate the complexities of digital transformation. By providing a well-rounded education on Industry 4.0 principles, technologies, and associated risks, OPs are empowered to lead and contribute effectively to the successful integration of Industry 4.0 within their organizations.

A novel approach to augment Industry 4.0 capabilities in Value Creation.

# Industry 4.0 Innovative Solutions

Operating Partners liaise with in-house technology advisors along with wide-access external subject matter expert advisors to identify I4.0 solutions to OpCo specific needs.

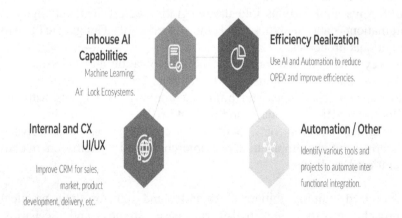

**Inhouse AI Capabilities**
Machine Learning,
Air Lock Ecosystems.

**Efficiency Realization**
Use AI and Automation to reduce OPEX and improve efficiencies.

**Internal and CX UI/UX**
Improve CRM for sales, market, product development, delivery, etc.

**Automation / Other**
Identify various tools and projects to automate inter functional integration.

# Venture Building Coaching and Support for OPs

It important to extend upskilling of innovation and adaptability by offering comprehensive training, primers, and support to Operating Partners (OPs) on integrating Venture Building Skills into their repertoire. In acknowledgment of the evolving landscape where startups and traditional businesses coalesce, such training initiatives empower OPs with the skills and tools necessary to spearhead in-house startup spin-offs or incubate Minimum Viable Products (MVPs).

The training curriculum should cover a range of crucial aspects, including ideation, prototype development, and strategic planning tailored specifically for in-house startups. OPs gain insights into the nuances of creating and nurturing innovative ventures within the established framework of portfolio companies. The focus extends to identifying opportunities for disruptive solutions, developing business models, and leveraging technology to create scalable and impactful ventures.

In addition to theoretical knowledge, such a specialized training incorporates practical applications and case studies, allowing OPs to engage with real-world scenarios. This experiential learning approach ensures that OPs are not only equipped with theoretical know-how but also possess the practical acumen to drive the successful incubation of startups within their portfolio companies.

Well planned primer sessions provide OPs with a deep dive into the Venture Building process, offering guidance on structuring, and managing in-house startup initiatives effectively. From validating ideas to assembling cross-functional teams, a purposeful primer equips OPs with the skills needed to navigate the intricacies of the startup ecosystem within the corporate setting.

Furthermore, ongoing support should extend beyond the training room, providing OPs with the necessary resources and mentorship to overcome challenges and capitalize on opportunities.

In essence, a PE commitment to in-housing Venture Building Skills development for OPs reflects a forward-looking dedication to fostering a culture of innovation and entrepreneurial thinking within the private equity landscape. By empowering OPs with the knowledge and tools needed to integrate startup principles into portfolio companies, they contribute to the creation of resilient, adaptive, and forward-thinking businesses in an ever-evolving market.

A novel concept of value creation through adapting corporate venture capital tools.

## The Venture Building Hub

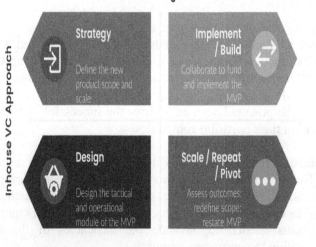

# The Quest for The Operating SuperPartner

## OP Talent Acquisition and Management

Identifying, recruiting, and retaining Operating Partners (OPs) is a shared pursuit for both Private Equity (PE) firms and Investment Management. It's a symbiotic relationship where the passion and dedication of OPs meet the constant challenges posed by an unceasing deal flow. Similarly, PE firms seek enduring partnerships with trial-tested OPs who consistently meet and exceed expectations. In essence, PE firms aspire to discover not just any partner, but a SuperPartner uniquely tailored to their needs. Importantly, SuperPartners are not merely found; they are crafted!

It requires the dedication of substantial effort and research to formulate a framework that not only identifies top OP talent but also advises PE firms and Investment Management on elevating their talent acquisition strategies. Recognizing and evaluating an OP involves scrutinizing four distinct criteria:

1. **Intrinsic Leadership**
2. **Technical Prowess**
3. **Track Record**
4. **The V-Factor**

Depending on the mandate's scope and scale, each criterion receives a weighted consideration to ensure a nuanced and tailored evaluation.

# Intrinsic Leadership: Beyond Skillsets to Character

Choosing OPs with the right personality traits is pivotal for success in private equity ventures. Insights from industry leaders and experts underscore specific key attributes:

1. **Visionary Leadership:**

   - *Description:* Exceptional OPs exhibit visionary leadership, inspiring teams with a compelling future-oriented vision.

   - *Impact:* Aligns the organization with strategic goals, fostering a sense of purpose and direction.

2. **Adaptability and Resilience:**

   - *Description:* Successful OPs embrace change, adapting to dynamic environments with resilience.

   - *Impact:* Navigates uncertainties and challenges, ensuring the ability to pivot strategies for optimal outcomes.

3. **Influential Communication:**

   - *Description:* OPs should communicate complex ideas with clarity, influencing diverse stakeholders.

   - *Impact:* Builds strong relationships, facilitates collaboration, and ensures a shared understanding of strategic objectives.

4. **Collaborative Approach:**

   - *Description:* Effective collaboration is a hallmark of successful OPs who collaborate seamlessly with diverse teams.

- *Impact:* Fosters teamwork, harnessing collective expertise for comprehensive value creation.

5. **Strategic Thinking and Decision-Making:**

   - *Description:* OPs exhibit strategic thinking, making well-informed decisions aligned with long-term goals.

   - *Impact:* Identifies and prioritizes value creation opportunities, steering the organization toward sustainable success.

6. **Adventurous Entrepreneurship:**

   - *Description:* Entrepreneurial spirit empowers OPs to take calculated risks and explore innovative solutions.

   - *Impact:* Drives innovation explores new avenues for growth and encourages a culture of continuous improvement.

7. **Empathy and Emotional Intelligence:**

   - *Description:* An empathetic approach and high emotional intelligence contribute to effective leadership.

   - *Impact:* Enhances team dynamics, fosters a positive workplace culture, and promotes employee engagement.

8. **Responsible Risk-Taking:**

   - *Description:* OPs assess risks judiciously, making informed decisions that balance risk and reward.

   - *Impact:* Ensures a proactive approach to risk management, safeguarding the organization's value.

9. **Passion for Continuous Learning:**

   - *Description:* OPs exhibit a passion for learning, staying informed about industry trends and best practices.

- *Impact:* Drives a culture of continuous improvement, positioning the organization at the forefront of industry developments.

10. **Results-Driven Accountability:**

- *Description:* A purposeful mindset ensures a commitment to achieving tangible outcomes.

- *Impact:* Enhances accountability, aligns actions with objectives, and drives the organization toward success.

These personality traits collectively contribute to the effectiveness of Operating Partners in navigating the complexities of private equity, fostering growth, and driving sustained value creation. Private equity firms benefit from selecting OPs who embody this combination of visionary leadership, adaptability, collaboration, and strategic acumen.

# Technical Prowess

Equally crucial is the identification of Operating Partners (OPs) with exceptionally advanced technical skill sets. It's essential to recognize that, although Ops collaborate extensively with business counterparts throughout the value creation process, they willingly take on the responsibility of initiating and auditing a substantial portion of the technical heavy lifting on their own. In stark contrast to PE deal teams, Ops operate independently, covering a significantly broader scope. To draw an analogy, if deal teams are akin to lions with their prides, Operating Partners are more like tigers, navigating and thriving on their own.

The key technical elements of an OP arsenal include:

1. **Financial Acumen:**

    - Description: Deep understanding of financial concepts, including financial modeling, valuation methods, and proficiency in analyzing financial statements.

    - Impact: Informed financial decision-making, accurate valuation assessments, and effective management of portfolio company finances.

2. **Strategic Vision:**

    - Description: Ability to develop and execute strategic initiatives aligned with the overall goals of the private equity firm, with an emphasis on value creation and long-term success.

    - Impact: Strategic growth, enhanced competitiveness, and sustained success of portfolio companies.

3. **Industry Expertise:**

    - Description: In-depth knowledge of the specific industry or industries in which the portfolio companies operate, allowing for informed decision-making and strategic guidance.

- Impact: Industry-specific insights leading to targeted and effective strategies, fostering growth and resilience.

4. **Operational Efficiency:**

- Description: Proficiency in identifying and implementing operational improvements to enhance efficiency, reduce costs, and optimize resource utilization within portfolio companies.

- Impact: Streamlined operations, improved profitability, and increased overall operational excellence.

5. **Deal Structuring Skills:**

- Description: Capability in structuring complex deals, negotiating terms, and assessing potential investment opportunities to ensure favorable outcomes for all stakeholders.

- Impact: Successful deal execution, favorable terms, and optimized investment structures.

6. **Risk Management:**

- Description: Ability to identify, assess, and mitigate risks associated with portfolio companies, ensuring that proactive measures are in place to protect and enhance value.

- Impact: Minimized risks, enhanced resilience, and protection of the portfolio's overall value.

7. **Technology Proficiency:**

- Description: Familiarity with emerging technologies and their potential impact on business operations, allowing for strategic adoption and integration of technology for growth.

- Impact: Strategic technological advancements, increased efficiency, and competitive positioning.

8. **Legal and Regulatory Compliance:**

    - Description: Knowledge of relevant legal and regulatory frameworks, ensuring that portfolio companies operate within compliance standards to avoid legal issues and reputational risks.

    - Impact: Mitigated legal risks, maintained compliance, and safeguarded the reputation of the portfolio.

9. **Communication and Negotiation Skills:**

    - Description: Effective communication and negotiation skills to build strong relationships with stakeholders, including investors, management teams, and external partners.

    - Impact: Positive stakeholder relationships, successful negotiations, and collaborative partnerships.

10. **Data-Driven Decision-Making:**

    - Description: A commitment to utilizing data analytics and metrics to inform decision-making processes, ensuring that strategic initiatives are based on empirical evidence and insights.

    - Impact: Informed decision-making, optimized strategies, and data-backed value creation initiatives.

These technical attributes collectively contribute to the operational success of an Operating Partner within the private equity landscape.

# Track Record

In selecting Operating Partners (OPs), evaluating their background and history is paramount. This encompasses their professional journey, industry experience, and past achievements. Here's an exploration of key considerations:

1. **Proven Industry Expertise**

   - Description: Evaluate the OP's depth of knowledge and experience within the relevant industry or sector.

   - Impact: Ensures the OP possesses insights critical for strategic decision-making, contributing to effective value creation.

2. **Track Record of Successful Engagements**

   - Description: Assess the OP's history of successful partnerships and engagements, especially within the private equity landscape.

   - Impact: Demonstrates a consistent ability to drive value and achieve positive outcomes, minimizing execution risks.

3. **Adaptability Across Industries**

   - Description: Consider the OP's ability to apply skills and insights across different industries or sectors.

   - Impact: Enhances versatility, enabling the OP to navigate diverse challenges and opportunities.

4. **Leadership in Transformational Initiatives**

   - Description: Examine instances where the OP played a pivotal role in leading transformative initiatives.

- Impact: Indicates a capacity for driving significant changes and innovation within portfolio companies.

5. **Financial Acumen and Deal Experience**

- Description: Evaluate the OP's financial acumen and experience in deal structuring and execution.

- Impact: Strengthens the OP's ability to align value creation strategies with financial objectives.

6. **Entrepreneurial Ventures**

- Description: Assess any entrepreneurial ventures or initiatives undertaken by the OP.

- Impact: Reflects an entrepreneurial mindset, contributing to a proactive approach in driving value.

7. **Global Experience and Network**

- Description: Consider whether the OP has a global perspective and an extensive professional network.

- Impact: Facilitates access to diverse resources and insights, valuable for international portfolios.

8. **Innovation and Technology Integration**

- Description: Evaluate the OP's inclination towards innovation and integration of technology in business.

- Impact: Ensures an adaptive approach to modern business challenges and opportunities.

9. **Operational Leadership Roles**

- Description: Review the OP's experience in operational leadership roles within companies.

- Impact: Demonstrates hands-on expertise in implementing operational improvements and efficiency measures.

## 10. Alignment with Fund Objectives

- Description: Ensure that the OP's background aligns with the specific objectives and focus areas of the private equity fund.

- Impact: Enhances synergy, ensuring the OP is well-aligned with the fund's strategic goals and expectations.

This comprehensive evaluation of an OP's background and history provides a holistic understanding of their capabilities, minimizing uncertainties and contributing to successful value creation within the private equity ecosystem.

# The V-Factor: Unleashing the Value Magicians

Among Operating Partners (OPs), the V-Factor, akin to the X-Factor, is the magical touch that sets extraordinary individuals apart. I would like to define the V-Factor as the Value Factor, encapsulating that elusive, surprising element that turns competent OPs into exceptional ones. It's the quality that makes them akin to magicians, not merely pulling rabbits from hats but willing to go down the rabbit hole if the hat or rabbit are taken away.

## Key Characteristics of the Value Factor

1. **Quasi-Eclectic Innovation:**

   - *Description:* OPs with the V-Factor possess a near-euphoric ability to conjure innovative solutions unexpectedly.

   - *Impact:* Injects an element of surprise into problem-solving, pushing beyond conventional boundaries for unparalleled outcomes.

2. **Bona Fide Problem Solvers:**

   - *Description:* Value Magicians don't just solve problems; they thrive on it. They approach challenges with an authentic commitment to finding unique and effective solutions.

   - *Impact:* Elevates the problem-solving process, turning hurdles into opportunities for unparalleled value creation.

3. **Rabbit-Hole Resilience:**

- *Description:* Similar to magicians persistently exploring the depths of their craft, OPs with the V-Factor delve into challenges with unwavering persistence.

- *Impact:* Ensures an unyielding pursuit of excellence, even when faced with the most intricate and convoluted business scenarios.

4. **Ownership Mentality:**

- *Description:* Those with the V-Factor don't just work for the business; they treat it as their own. An inherent sense of ownership fuels their dedication.

- *Impact:* Drives a level of commitment that goes beyond conventional professional roles, fostering a profound connection to the success of the enterprise.

5. **Unstoppable Drive:**

- *Description:* OPs with the Value Factor cannot be stopped. Their relentless drive and passion fuel an unstoppable force that propels them toward overcoming challenges.

- *Impact:* Inspires teams, creating a dynamic environment where hurdles are viewed as stepping stones to greater achievements.

# Harnessing the V-Factor for Optimal Impact

Recognizing and nurturing the V-Factor in OPs is about more than talent acquisition; it's about unlocking the full spectrum of potential within an individual. An ambitious OP head-hunting approach involves identifying, cultivating, and empowering the V-Factor into, ensuring that the above-and-beyond actions they bring to the table becomes a consistent and transformative force in the private equity landscape. The V-Factor isn't just a trait; it's a catalyst for innovation, resilience, and unparalleled value creation. Real-Life Examples of Ops with the V-Factor

| Operating Partner | V-Factor Highlight | Success Story |
|---|---|---|
| **Ram Charan** | Renowned for transformative insights and diagnosing business challenges. | Served as an Operating Partner, leading the turnaround of a struggling manufacturing portfolio company. Introduced innovative operational models, saving the company, and driving substantial profitability. |
| **Sheryl Palmer** | Recognized for visionary leadership and innovative approaches to sustainable growth. | As an Operating Partner, redefined the growth trajectory of a real estate-focused private equity portfolio. Introduced progressive sustainability initiatives and technological integrations, transforming the portfolio into a modern, environmentally conscious real estate beacon. |
| **David N. Miller** | Celebrated for relentless pursuit of excellence and commitment to operational efficiency. | Demonstrated the V-Factor in a healthcare-focused private equity engagement. His operational restructuring optimized costs and significantly enhanced patient care quality. Miller's firsthand approach set a new standard for operational performance within the healthcare portfolio. |

**214**

# Operating SuperPartner Alphas

While the dominance of "alpha personalities" among Operating Partners (OPs) in the private equity landscape can not me scientifically confirmed, certain characteristics commonly associated with alpha personalities may align well with the traits sought in successful OPs.

Ideally an Alpha Super Operating Partner (ASOP) needs to be a "Cladie" (think Iron Clad):

1. Confidence:

2. Leadership

3. Assertiveness

4. Decisiveness

5. Influence

6. Edge

# The Merit-based OP Assessment Toolkit

| Element | Comments | Exceptional | Above Average | Average | Low | N/A |
|---|---|---|---|---|---|---|
| **Personality** | | | | | | |
| Visionary Leadership | | ☐ | ☐ | ☐ | ☐ | ☐ |
| Adaptability and Resilience | | ☐ | ☐ | ☐ | ☐ | ☐ |
| Influential Communication | | ☐ | ☐ | ☐ | ☐ | ☐ |
| Collaborative Approach | | ☐ | ☐ | ☐ | ☐ | ☐ |
| Strategic Thinking and Decision-Making | | ☐ | ☐ | ☐ | ☐ | ☐ |
| Adventurous Entrepreneurship | | ☐ | ☐ | ☐ | ☐ | ☐ |
| Empathy and Emotional Intelligence | | ☐ | ☐ | ☐ | ☐ | ☐ |
| **Technical** | | | | | | |
| Financial Acumen | | ☐ | ☐ | ☐ | ☐ | ☐ |
| Strategic Vision | | ☐ | ☐ | ☐ | ☐ | ☐ |
| Industry Expertise | | ☐ | ☐ | ☐ | ☐ | ☐ |
| Operational Efficiency | | ☐ | ☐ | ☐ | ☐ | ☐ |
| Deal Structuring Skills | | ☐ | ☐ | ☐ | ☐ | ☐ |
| Risk Management | | ☐ | ☐ | ☐ | ☐ | ☐ |
| Technology Proficiency | | ☐ | ☐ | ☐ | ☐ | ☐ |
| **Track Record** | | | | | | |

| | | | | | |
|---|---|---|---|---|---|
| Proven Industry Expertise | ☐ | ☐ | ☐ | ☐ | ☐ |
| Track Record of Successful Engagements | ☐ | ☐ | ☐ | ☐ | ☐ |
| Adaptability Across Industries | ☐ | ☐ | ☐ | ☐ | ☐ |
| Leadership in Transformational Initiatives | ☐ | ☐ | ☐ | ☐ | ☐ |
| Financial Acumen and Deal Experience | ☐ | ☐ | ☐ | ☐ | ☐ |
| Entrepreneurial Ventures | ☐ | ☐ | ☐ | ☐ | ☐ |
| Global Experience and Network | ☐ | ☐ | ☐ | ☐ | ☐ |
| **Value Factor** | ☐ | ☐ | ☐ | ☐ | ☐ |
| **Alpha Traits** | | | | | |
| Confidence | ☐ | ☐ | ☐ | ☐ | ☐ |
| Leadership | ☐ | ☐ | ☐ | ☐ | ☐ |
| Assertiveness | ☐ | ☐ | ☐ | ☐ | ☐ |
| Decisiveness | ☐ | ☐ | ☐ | ☐ | ☐ |
| Influence | ☐ | ☐ | ☐ | ☐ | ☐ |
| Edge | ☐ | ☐ | ☐ | ☐ | ☐ |

# Fit For Purpose vs. Designed for Growth

*"Not all Operating Companies (OpCos) are Born Equal!"*

The strategic orientation of Operating Companies (OpCos) plays a crucial role in understanding the difference between "Fit for Purpose" and "Designed for Growth" OpCos; this discrimination is essential for effective leadership. In many cases, PE firms accept the fact that a certain OpCo is good in its current form—either it is not worth the extra effort or simply "if it's not broken, don't fix it." So, due to no short-sightedness or complacency of the OP, the mandate is to harvest value and not undertake a major organizational value chain (OVC) change. Simply put, that OpCo is "Fit for Purpose" by choice. The OP needs to establish early on what mode or game is in play and plan resources accordingly. In many cases, OP might or need to establish the mandate to transform the business from one mode to another.

| Criteria | Fit For Purpose OpCo | Designed for Growth OpCo |
|---|---|---|
| **Strategic Focus** | Operational efficiency and market consolidation. | Market expansion, innovation, and rapid scalability. |
| **Key Characteristics** | - Operational Efficiency | - Market Expansion |
| | - Niche Market Focus | - Innovation |
| | - Stability | - Scalability |
| | - Defensive Strategy | - Offensive Strategy |
| **Operating Partner's Role** | - Operational Optimization | - Market Entry Strategy |
| | - Market Consolidation | - Innovation Leadership |
| | - Risk Management | - Scalability Planning |
| | | - M&A and Partnership Exploration |

Operating Partners in private equity firms need to tailor their strategies based on the nature of the portfolio company. Fit For Purpose OpCos require a focus on stability and efficiency, while Designed for Growth OpCos demand a dynamic approach toward expansion and innovation.

In essence, the strategic orientation of OpCos significantly influences the role of Operating Partners. Whether fine-tuning existing operations or spearheading growth initiatives, OPs play a pivotal role in aligning strategies with the unique demands of each OpCo, contributing to the overall success of the portfolio.

# Long-Term Incentive Plans (LTIPs) for Operating Partners

*"The Essence of Private Equity Honey: what makes honey, craves honey!"*

Attracting and retaining top talent is crucial for driving value creation within portfolio companies. One instrumental tool in achieving this is the implementation of Long-Term Incentive Plans (LTIPs) tailored for Operating Partners, C-Suite executives, and key staff. Among the various forms of LTIPs, vesting equity interest emerges as a compelling incentive, fostering alignment of interests between executives and investors while ensuring sustained commitment and performance.

Vesting equity interest is a distinctive form of LTIP that grants individuals a stake in the ownership and success of a company over an extended period. This structure is designed to reward long-term commitment, strategic vision, and operational excellence, crucial elements in the private equity value creation journey. The vesting period typically spans several years, ensuring that executives remain actively engaged in the company's growth and performance.

# Forms of Vesting Equity Interest

| Type of LTIP | Overview | Advantages | Considerations |
|---|---|---|---|
| **Restricted Stock Units (RSUs)** | RSUs represent a promise to deliver shares of company stock after a specified vesting period. Unlike stock options, RSUs carry no exercise price. | RSUs are straightforward and align executives' interests with stock price performance, as the value is tied to the company's market value. | Tax implications arise upon vesting, requiring careful financial planning. |
| **Phantom Shares** | Phantom shares are units that mirror the value of actual company shares but do not grant ownership. Executives receive cash or equivalent upon vesting. | Provides flexibility in cash or stock settlement, allowing for customization based on executives' preferences. | The absence of actual equity ownership may impact the psychological link between executives and shareholders. |

# Key Elements of LTIP Design

| Design Element | Description |
|---|---|
| **Performance Metrics** | Clearly defined and measurable performance metrics are crucial. These may include financial targets, operational milestones, or specific value creation goals aligned with the private equity firm's strategy. |
| **Vesting Schedule** | The vesting period should be strategically determined to encourage sustained commitment. Common structures include cliff vesting, graded vesting, or a combination of both. |
| **Alignment with Exit Strategies** | LTIPs should align with the private equity firm's exit strategy, ensuring that executives share in the success realized at the time of exit or IPO. |

# LTIP Considerations for Private Equity Firms

| Consideration | Description |
|---|---|
| **Customization** | LTIPs should be tailored to the specific goals and challenges of the portfolio company, reflecting the unique aspects of its industry, growth trajectory, and risk profile. |
| **Communication and Transparency** | Clear communication regarding LTIP terms, performance expectations, and potential outcomes is essential to foster trust and commitment among executives. |
| **Legal and Regulatory Compliance** | Compliance with local and international regulations, tax implications, and legal considerations is paramount. Seeking legal counsel ensures that LTIPs adhere to relevant laws. |

Incentivizing Operating Partners through vesting equity interest within LTIPs is a strategic imperative for private equity firms aiming to maximize value creation. By carefully designing these plans, aligning them with the firm's objectives, and addressing legal and regulatory considerations, private equity firms can create a powerful tool that motivates and retains top talent, ultimately driving success in their portfolio companies.

# Additional Forms of LTIPs: Stock Options and More

*Key Advantages:* Alignment with Stock Performance: Options align the interests of executives with stock price performance, as their value is tied to the appreciation of the company's stock.

*Considerations:* Options are subject to a vesting period, and executives gain the right to exercise them gradually over time. The exercise price is predetermined and should be carefully set to provide a meaningful incentive without being too burdensome for executives.

| Type of LTIP | Overview |
| --- | --- |
| Stock Options | Stock options provide the holder with the right to purchase a specified number of company shares at a predetermined exercise price (strike price) within a defined period. |
| Employee Stock Purchase Plans (ESPPs) | While not a traditional form of LTIP, ESPPs allow employees, including executives, to purchase company stock at a discounted price. ESPPs often operate over shorter periods and can complement other LTIPs. |
| Performance Share Units (PSUs) | PSUs are similar to RSUs but tie vesting to the achievement of specific performance goals. Executives receive shares based on the company's performance against predetermined metrics. |
| Stock Appreciation Rights (SARs) | SARs provide executives with the right to receive the appreciation in the company's stock value over a predetermined period. They are settled in cash or stock. |
| Employee Stock Ownership Plans (ESOPs) | ESOPs are broader programs where employees, including executives, become beneficial owners of shares in the company over time. This form emphasizes broader employee ownership. |

*Choosing the Right LTIP:* When selecting the appropriate LTIP, private equity firms should consider the company's objectives, the desired level of ownership alignment, tax implications, and the preferences of key executives. Combining different LTIP forms or implementing a tiered approach can also be effective in addressing the diverse needs of executives within the organization.

# The Efficiency and Potency of the LTIP

There are two key factors that define how efficient and potent is the LTIP:

- Efficiency: The Reward-to-Cost Ratio
- Potency: The Value Creation to Executive Reward Ratio

# The Reward-to-Cost Ratio

In the context of executive compensation, specifically Long-Term Incentive Plans (LTIPs), this ratio measures the value executives gain from an LTIP compared to the cost incurred by the company in implementing and maintaining the plan.

The formula for the Reward-to-Cost Ratio is typically expressed as follows:

*R/C Ratio= Total Cost Incurred by the Company / Total Value Realized by Executives*

In this formula:

- Total Value Realized by Executives includes the value of vested shares, exercised options, or any other benefits derived from the LTIP.

- Total Cost Incurred by the Company encompasses the expenses associated with designing, implementing, and managing the LTIP, including the accounting costs, administrative expenses, and any other related costs.

A high Reward-to-Cost Ratio suggests that the company is efficiently using its resources to generate value for executives, shareholders, and the overall organization. Conversely, a lower ratio may indicate that the LTIP is not delivering a proportionate return on the investment made by the company.

Example:

1. **Total Value Realized by Executives:**
   - Executive A receives vested shares worth $2 million.
   - Executive B exercises stock options with a value of $1.5 million.

Total Value Realized=$2 million+$1.5 million=$3.5 million

2. **Total Cost Incurred by the Company:**
   - Designing and implementing the LTIP: $500,000
   - Administrative expenses: $200,000
   - Other related costs: $100,000

Total Cost Incurred=$500,000+$200,000+$100,000=$800,000

3. **Reward-to-Cost Ratio:**
R/C Ratio=$3.5 million/ $800,000$R$
R/C Ratio≈4.375

Interpretation: In this example, the Reward-to-Cost Ratio is approximately 4.375. This suggests that for every dollar spent by the company on the LTIP, executives realized a return of $4.375. A higher ratio like this may indicate that the LTIP is providing substantial value relative to the cost incurred by the company in implementing the plan

.

# The Value Creation to Executive Reward Ratio

The "Value Creation to Executive Reward Ratio" or "Company Upside to Executive Value Ratio." This ratio is calculated by dividing the upside or value created by the company (e.g., increase in market capitalization or enterprise value) by the total value given to executives who vested their LTIP.

**Formula:**

Value Creation to Executive Reward Ratio  =  Company Upside  / Total Value Given to Vested Executives

**Interpretation:**

- If the ratio is greater than 1, it indicates that the company generated more value than the total value given to executives, suggesting a positive return on the LTIP investment.

- If the ratio is less than 1, it suggests that the company's value creation was less than the total value provided to executives, and further analysis may be needed to assess the effectiveness of the LTIP.

---

Example:
Let's say a company's market capitalization increased by $17.5 million during the LTIP vesting period, and the total value given to executives who vested their LTIP was $3.5 million.

Add expenses (as in previous example)
Value Creation to Executive Reward Ratio=$17.5    million/ ($3.5 million + 0.8 million) = 4.07x

In this example, the ratio is 4x, indicating that, for every dollar spent on executives through the LTIP, the company created $4 in market capitalization.

---

# Endnote

## Navigating the Pathways of Value Creation

Dear Esteemed Reader,

As this guide reaches its conclusion, I'm enveloped by a deep sense of gratitude. Your choice to join me in traversing the intricate world of Private Equity, through the lens of operational partnerships and total value creation, has been both an honor and a privilege. This book, a mosaic of insights, frameworks, and stories, is a shared expedition towards unravelling the complexities and mastering the essence of creating enduring value in the dynamic sphere of Private Equity.

The creation of this work was driven by a desire to illuminate the often-obscure paths of Private Equity, to offer a beacon for those navigating its challenges, and to demystify the roles and impact of Operating Partners. However, this journey has been as much a revelation for me as I hope it will be for you. In articulating my perspectives, I've confronted my own vulnerabilities, re-examined my experiences, and above all, embraced the privilege of contributing to our collective understanding of value creation.

Your willingness to invest your time into these pages has been my greatest motivation. Whether you stand as a veteran in the Private Equity realm or are just stepping onto the path of value creation, it is your pursuit of knowledge, excellence, and innovation that will ultimately redefine the contours of this industry.

This book was penned with the aspiration not merely to inform but to inspire and to provoke deeper contemplation on the intricacies of operational excellence, and transformative leadership within Private Equity. The journey of value creation is as much about the tangible impacts we forge as it is about the personal evolutions we undergo. The frameworks, anecdotes, and strategies shared herein are merely guides on a journey that is intimately your own.

To every reader who has bestowed upon me the gift of their time and the openness of their perspective, please receive my heartfelt appreciation. Your engagement signifies more than support for this narrative; it reflects a commitment to the noble endeavor of shaping the future through strategic value creation.

As we part ways at this juncture, I encourage you to remember that the quest for value creation is an endless journey of discovery, innovation, and, fundamentally, contribution to the broader tapestry of our professional and personal lives. The world is in need of visionaries who not only excel in financial acumen but also champion the growth, sustainability, and resilience of their enterprises and communities.

May this book be a milestone on your voyage towards mastering the art of value creation in Private Equity. May your path be marked by relentless growth, impactful achievements, and the fulfillment derived from unlocking the potential within yourselves and those you guide.

With the deepest respect and best wishes for your continued journey,


Mohamad Chahine

# Selected Glossary

1. **mVMS** - Merit-driven Value Management System

2. **TVC** - Total Value Creation

3. **mOM** – Merit-based Operating Model

4. **mOPP** – Merit-driven Operating Partner Playbook

5. **BVC** - Balanced ValueCard

6. **VEF** - Value Engine Flywheel

7. **PEMVR** - PUSH Excellence Make Value Right

8. **OPEO** - The Operating Partner Executive Officer

9. **OVC** - Operational Value Creation

10. **POPP** - Portfolio Optimization and Periodization Process

11. **SSOF** - Scale and Scope Optimization Framework

12. **Investomer**:  A congruent stakeholder - between Customer and Investor

13. **mVA -** The Merit-Driven Value Accelerator – A Cheat Sheet for the mVMS

14. **OP 4.0** – OP Industry 4.0 – ready

15. **PMO** – Project Management Office

**232**

Made in United States
North Haven, CT
22 April 2024